Building RESTful Web Services with PHP 7

Lumen, Composer, API testing, Microservices, and more

Haafiz Waheed-ud-din Ahmad

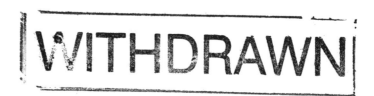

BIRMINGHAM - MUMBAI

Building RESTful Web Services with PHP 7

First published: September 2017

Production reference: 1060917

Published by Packt Publishing Ltd.
Livery Place
35 Livery Street
Birmingham
B3 2PB, UK.

ISBN 978-1-78712-774-6

www.packtpub.com

Credits

Author
Haafiz Waheed-ud-din Ahmad

Reviewer
Shuvankar Sarkar

Commissioning Editor
Aaron Lazar

Acquisition Editor
Chaitanya Nair

Content Development Editor
Zeeyan Pinheiro

Technical Editors
Ketan Kamble

Copy Editor
Sameen Siddiqui

Project Coordinator
Vaidehi Sawant

Proofreader
Safis Editing

Indexer
Francy Puthiry

Graphics
Abhinash Sahu

Production Coordinator
Nilesh Mohite

About the Author

Haafiz Waheed-ud**-din Ahmad** has been working in the IT industry since 2008. He has mostly worked in web application development and mostly used PHP at the server side. Although most of his experience is in PHP, he is a technology agnostic person and also likes to learn and adapt to new technologies. He also acts as an adviser for startups and new developers.

He has worked on Python and JavaScript as well. He likes to experiment with new technologies, and he has also explored Golang, Scala, and Neo4J. He also has a keen interest in data science and big data domain and has worked on D3.js for data visualization. He is not just a technology enthusiast but also likes to solve day-to-day problems by the usage of technology. He blogs at `http://haafiz.me/`. You can follow him on twitter at `@Haafiz786`.

About the Reviewer

Shuvankar Sarkar is an IT Analyst experienced in C#, .NET, PHP, and web development. He is a technology enthusiast and maintains a blog at `http://shuvankar.com`. You can follow him on Twitter at `@sonu041`. Shuvankar is interested in computer security as well.

I would like to thank my family for making my life easy and full of happiness.

www.PacktPub.com

For support files and downloads related to your book, please visit www.PacktPub.com.

Did you know that Packt offers eBook versions of every book published, with PDF and ePub files available? You can upgrade to the eBook version at www.PacktPub.com and as a print book customer, you are entitled to a discount on the eBook copy. Get in touch with us at service@packtpub.com for more details.

At www.PacktPub.com, you can also read a collection of free technical articles, sign up for a range of free newsletters and receive exclusive discounts and offers on Packt books and eBooks.

https://www.packtpub.com/mapt

Get the most in-demand software skills with Mapt. Mapt gives you full access to all Packt books and video courses, as well as industry-leading tools to help you plan your personal development and advance your career.

Why subscribe?

- Fully searchable across every book published by Packt
- Copy and paste, print, and bookmark content
- On demand and accessible via a web browser

Customer Feedback

Thanks for purchasing this Packt book. At Packt, quality is at the heart of our editorial process. To help us improve, please leave us an honest review on this book's Amazon page at https://www.amazon.com/dp/B075CK8S7D.

If you'd like to join our team of regular reviewers, you can e-mail us at customerreviews@packtpub.com. We award our regular reviewers with free eBooks and videos in exchange for their valuable feedback. Help us be relentless in improving our products!

Table of Contents

Preface

Web services has always been an important topic. With REST, things became simpler and better. Nowadays, RESTful web services are widely used. It was important a decade ago, but **Single Page Applications** (**SPAs**) and mobile applications have increased its usage greatly. The aim of this book is to educate PHP developers about the RESTful web services architecture, the current tools available to efficiently create RESTful web services such as a micro-framework named Lumen, automated API testing, the API testing framework, security and microservices architecture.

Although this book is specific to PHP as we will be building RESTful web services in PHP7, it is neither just about PHP7 nor just about REST. RESTful web services and implementation in PHP is what we do in this book. However, you will learn a lot more than that. You will learn about some PHP features that are new in PHP7. We will cover how we should structure our application and some common threats with respect to the web and web services. You will learn how to improve a basic RESTful web service and understand the importance of testing and the different types of testing. So it is not about just REST or PHP, but also about some minor but important programming-related stuff that is simple but makes things a lot better in the real world. At the end of this book, you will learn about an architecture named microservices.

In other words, although this book is intended for PHP developers, it will benefit them beyond just PHP. So, this book is not a cookbook, but a journey in which you start learning about RESTful webservices and PHP7 and then start building RESTful web services. You can then keep improving your RESTful web services by learning about the problems in it and fixing those. During such improvements, you will learn the different things in PHP and benefit even beyond PHP.

What this book covers

Chapter 1, *RESTful Web Services, Introduction and Motivation*, introduces you to web services, REST architecture, the RESTful web services, and its comparison to other web services such as HTTP verbs and RESTful endpoints. It also explains web services through the example of a blog and then talk about the response format and response code.

Chapter 2, *PHP7, To Code It Better*, includes new features and changes in PHP7 that we will either use in this book or are very important and worth discussing.

Chapter 3, *Creating RESTful Endpoints*, is about creating REST API endpoints for CRUD operations of a blog post in Vanilla PHP. It also explains the manual way of testing API endpoints through a REST client named Postman.

Chapter 4, *Reviewing Design Flaws and Security Threats*, reviews what we have built in the preceding chapter and highlights the problems and flaws in it so that we can improvise later.

Chapter 5, *Load and Resolve with Composer*, an Evolutionary, is about an evolutionary tool in the PHP ecosystem: composer. This is not just an autoloader or package installer, but a dependency manager. So, you will learn about composer in this chapter.

Chapter 6, *Illuminating RESTful Web Services with Lumen*, introduces you to a micro-framework named Lumen, in which we will rewrite our RESTful web services endpoints and review how this tool will significantly improve our speed and application structure.

Chapter 7, *Improving RESTful Web Services*, equips us to improve what we did in the preceding chapter; you will learn how to improve RESTful web services. We will create authentication and make a Transformer to separate how JSON structure should look. Also, we will improve in terms of security and learn about SSL.

Chapter 8, *API Testing – Guards on the Gates*, introduces the need of automated tests. Will introduce different type of tests and then focus on API testing. We will then cover an automated testing framework named CodeCeption and write API tests in it.

Chapter 9, *Microservices*, is about the microservices architecture. We will understand the benefits and challenges of microservices and look into some of possible solutions and trade-offs.

What you need for this book

Although I used Ubuntu, any operating system with PHP7 installed on it will work fine. The only thing required other than PHP7 will be an RDBMS. This book uses MySQL-related settings when connecting to database, so MySQL is ideal, but MariaDB or PostgreSQL will also be fine.

Who this book is for

This book is written for the following audience:

- Anyone who has some basic PHP knowledge and wants to build RESTful web services.
- Developers who know basic PHP and have developed a basic dynamic website and want to build a RESTful web service.
- Developers who have learned PHP and worked mostly in open source CMS, such as WordPress, and want to move toward developing custom applications where a web service needs to be built.
- Developers who are stuck with legacy systems done in Code Igniter and want to explore the modern ecosystem of PHP.
- Developers who have used modern frameworks such as Yii or Laravel, but are not sure about the critical pieces required to build the REST API that not only serves the purpose but works well in the long run, something that doesn't always need manual testing and is maintainable and extendable.
- Seasoned PHP developers who have created a very basic API that returns data but want to make themselves familiar with how it should be done according to REST standards, how it will work when authentication comes into the picture, and how to write tests for it.

Conventions

In this book, you will find a number of text styles that distinguish between different kinds of information. Here are some examples of these styles and an explanation of their meaning.

Code words in text, database table names, folder names, filenames, file extensions, pathnames, dummy URLs, user input, and Twitter handles are shown as follows: "The `randGen()` method takes two parameters defining the range of the returned value."

A block of code is set as follows:

```php
<?php
function add($num1, $num2):int{
    return ($num1+$num2);
}

echo add(2,4); //6
echo add(2.5,4); //6
```

When we wish to draw your attention to a particular part of a code block, the relevant lines or items are set in bold:

```php
<?php
function add($num1, $num2):int{
    return ($num1+$num2);
}

echo add(2,4); //6
echo add(2.5,4); //6
```

Any command-line input or output is written as follows:

```
sudo add-apt-repository ppa:ondrej/php
```

New terms and **important words** are shown in bold. Words that you see on the screen, for example, in menus or dialog boxes, appear in the text.

 Warnings or important notes appear like this.

 Tips and tricks appear like this.

Reader feedback

Feedback from our readers is always welcome. Let us know what you think about this book-what you liked or disliked. Reader feedback is important for us as it helps us develop titles that you will really get the most out of. To send us general feedback, simply e-mail feedback@packtpub.com, and mention the book's title in the subject of your message. If there is a topic that you have expertise in and you are interested in either writing or contributing to a book, see our author guide at www.packtpub.com/authors.

Downloading the example code

You can download the example code files for this book from your account at
`http://www.packtpub.com`. If you purchased this book elsewhere, you can visit
`http://www.packtpub.com/support` and register to have the files e-mailed directly to you.
You can download the code files by following these steps:

1. Log in or register to our website using your e-mail address and password.
2. Hover the mouse pointer on the **SUPPORT** tab at the top.
3. Click on **Code Downloads & Errata**.
4. Enter the name of the book in the **Search** box.
5. Select the book for which you're looking to download the code files.
6. Choose from the drop-down menu where you purchased this book from.
7. Click on **Code Download**.

Once the file is downloaded, please make sure that you unzip or extract the folder using the latest version of:

- WinRAR / 7-Zip for Windows
- Zipeg / iZip / UnRarX for Mac
- 7-Zip / PeaZip for Linux

The code bundle for the book is also hosted on GitHub at
`https://github.com/PacktPublishing/Building-RESTful-Web-Services-with-PHP-7`. We
also have other code bundles from our rich catalog of books and videos available at
`https://github.com/PacktPublishing/`. Check them out!

Errata

Although we have taken every care to ensure the accuracy of our content, mistakes do happen. If you find a mistake in one of our books-maybe a mistake in the text or the code-we would be grateful if you could report this to us. By doing so, you can save other readers from frustration and help us improve subsequent versions of this book. If you find any errata, please report them by visiting `http://www.packtpub.com/submit-errata`, selecting your book, clicking on the **Errata Submission Form** link, and entering the details of your errata. Once your errata are verified, your submission will be accepted and the errata will be uploaded to our website or added to any list of existing errata under the Errata section of that title. To view the previously submitted errata, go to
`https://www.packtpub.com/books/content/support` and enter the name of the book in the search field. The required information will appear under the **Errata** section.

Piracy

Piracy of copyrighted material on the Internet is an ongoing problem across all media. At Packt, we take the protection of our copyright and licenses very seriously. If you come across any illegal copies of our works in any form on the Internet, please provide us with the location address or website name immediately so that we can pursue a remedy. Please contact us at copyright@packtpub.com with a link to the suspected pirated material. We appreciate your help in protecting our authors and our ability to bring you valuable content.

Questions

If you have a problem with any aspect of this book, you can contact us at questions@packtpub.com, and we will do our best to address the problem.

1
RESTful Web Services, Introduction and Motivation

RESTful web services are being used widely nowadays. RESTful is simple and most widely used among other web services. In fact, its simplicity is a reason for its fame as well. If you are reading this book, then chances are that you know something about RESTful web services. You probably have used it or you have just heard of it. But even if you don't know much about RESTful web services, don't worry as we are first defining it right here. So first, let's list the high level topics that we will be covering in this chapter:

- Web services, what is a web service?
- REST architecture (constraints of REST)
- RESTful web services
- Conventions of RESTful web services
- HTTP verbs (methods)
- Why RESTful web services?
- Response type and response codes
- Case study - RESTful web service endpoints for a blog

However, there are a lot of misconceptions about RESTful web services. For example, some people think that anything over the web returning JSON is a RESTful web service and RESTful web services only return JSON. This is not true.

In fact, RESTful web services support multiple formats and not everything returning JSON is a RESTful web service. To avoid confusion, let us understand what RESTful web service is.

A web service based on the REST architecture is a RESTful web service. So, what exactly is a web service and REST architecture? Let's start by understanding web service first and then the REST architecture.

Web services

Web services are defined differently at different places. Word-by word translation states that any service provided on the web including a web page is a web service but this isn't true if the technical term *web service* is referred to.

To define web service, we will look at web service definition from the W3C glossary:

> *"A Web service is a software system designed to support inter-operable machine-to-machine interaction over a network. It has an interface described in a machine-process able format (specifically WSDL). Other systems interact with the Web service in a manner prescribed by its description using SOAP-messages, typically conveyed using HTTP with an XML serialization in conjunction with other Web-related standards." -W3C, web services glossary.*

This definition again, is not completely true as it is more specific to SOAP and WSDL based web services. In fact, later in the W3C Working Group Note, February 11, 2004, it was stated that:

> *"We can identify two major classes of web services:*
> *- REST-compliant web services, in which the primary purpose of the service is to manipulate XML representations of Web resources using a uniform set of "stateless" operations;*
> *- and arbitrary web services, in which the service may expose an arbitrary set of operations."*

So considering that, a more general and better definition of a web service is this, from the preceding mentioned W3C web services glossary definition:

> *"A Web service is a software system designed to support inter-operable machine-to-machine interaction over a network."*

Why a web service?

Now, we know what a web service is. So before proceeding to REST, it is important to know the need for a web service. Where can a web service be used?

As just defined, a web service is a system to support machine-to-machine inter-operable communication over a network. It is very useful for communication between different systems or devices. In our case, we will be using web services to provide an interface by which either a mobile application or a web application will be able to communicate with a server to get and store data. This will make the client-side application separate from the server side logic. And nowadays, SPAs (Single Page Applications) and mobile applications need to be stand alone, separate from server side and only interacting with server side logic with web services. So definitely web services are very much important nowadays. However, web service usage is not limited to client side application usage but it is also useful in server to server communication where one server acts as a client.

REST architecture

REST stands for Representational State Transfer. It is an architectural style founded by Roy Fielding in 2000 and was stated in his PhD dissertation. He stated that REST *"provides a set of architectural constraints that, when applied as a whole, emphasizes scalability of component interactions, generality of interfaces, independent deployment of components, and intermediary components to reduce interaction latency, enforce security, and encapsulate legacy systems."*.

REST is an architectural style for a network-based application and HTTP 1.1 was based on it, as it was developed in parallel to HTTP 1.1.

A RESTful system or RESTful web service must abide by the following six constraints; otherwise, it will not be considered as RESTful or REST-compliant. While reading and understanding the following mentioned constraints, think about the modern web as an example of REST architecture.

Client server

REST is about separating the client and server. This constraint is about "separation of concerns". It means that the server and client have separate responsibilities, so one is not responsible for the other's duties. For example, the client is not responsible for data storage on the server as it is the server's responsibility. In the same way, the server doesn't need to know about the user interface. So both the server and client perform their tasks and fulfill their own responsibilities which makes their work easier. Hence, the server can be more scalable and the user interface on the client can be independent and more interactive.

Stateless

Client server communication is stateless. Each request coming from the client will have all the information required to serve a request. This means there is no state in this communication other than what is in the request. The response which the client will get will be based on the request without looking at any state other than what is in request.

If the session needs to be maintained, the session will be stored based on a token or identifier which is coming in the request. So if we look at an example of a web request, then the flow of HTTP is no more than a request sent by the **client** to the **server** and a response, sent back to the **client** from the **server,** as shown in the following diagram:

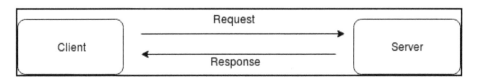

If a session needs to be maintained, the session data will be stored on the server, while the session identifier will be sent back to the client. In subsequent requests, the client will include that session identifier in every request by which the server will identify the client and load the related session's data as explained in the following diagram:

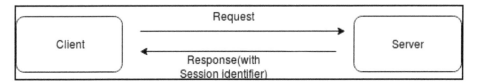

And in subsequent requests:

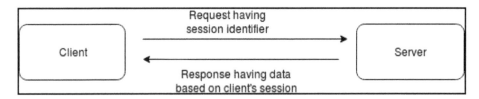

So REST is stateless. To maintain the state, one needs to pass an identifier or any other information, to logically group different requests to maintain a session in the request. If no such identifier is passed in the request, the server will never know if those two requests are from same client.

The advantage of statelessness is simplicity. The same requests will not result in different responses unless the request parameters are changed. It will return different results based on different request parameters not due to some sort of state. Even the state depends on requests, as shown in the preceding example. So that session identifier is in the request, which can result in a different state and, hence, results in a different response.

Cache-able

This constraint specifies that a RESTful web service response must define itself as cacheable or not, so that the client can know whether it should be cached or not. If it is correctly defined, it can result in less overhead and better performance because the client will not go to the server if it is able to use the cached version.

Uniform interface

The uniform interface is the most distinguishing constraint. It basically decouples the architecture makes the interface separate from the implementation, just as any good system does.

It is similar to how it is in OOP: an interface separates the implementation and declaration. It is similar to how an operating system separates the user interface from the complex implementation logic that keeps our software's running.

The uniform interface has four constraints. In order to understand uniform interface, we need to understand these constraints.

Resource identification

Resources will be identified in requests. For example, a resource in a web-based REST system will be identified by the URI. And no matter how a resource is stored on the server, it will remain separate from what will be returned to the client in the response.

In fact, resource storage on the server is an implementation but the request and response is what a client is interacting with, so it is like an interface to the client. And a client can identify a resource by this interface. So all that a client knows is what it is requesting and getting in response.

For example, a client usually sends a request to the URI and gets a response in the form of HTML, JSON, or XML. None of these formats are how the server stores data internally in the database or somewhere else on the server. But for a client, it is the URI where it will hit and the HTML, JSON, and XML is what it gets.

This is what a resource is for a client, no matter how it is stored on the server. And this is the benefit, because no matter if the server's internal logic or representation is changed, for the client it will remain the same because the client sends the request to the URI and gets a response in the form of HTML, JSON, or XML and not how it is stored on the server. This constraint, results in loose coupling of resource identification and representation.

Manipulation of resources through representations

This constraint states that the client should hold the representation of a resource that has enough information to modify or delete the resource. For example, in the web-based REST system, any operation can be performed on a resource using the HTTP method and URI. This makes things easy to follow, as the API developer doesn't need to provide documentation for each and every endpoint related to a resource.

Self-descriptive messages

This constraint states that each message should be able to be processed based on information contained in itself. That means, every message passed between the server and client should be stateless be independent of other messages. One message doesn't have an impact on other messages. So, it doesn't matter if two messages are passed in some particular order or not, as they are independent. The request in a message is enough to get a response and that response has all that needs to be conveyed.

Hypermedia as the engine of application state (HATEOAS)

This constraint states that, based on what a server provides to a REST client, the REST client should be able to discover all available actions and resources. In other words, it states that if a client knows an entry point then from that first endpoint, it should be able to discover other relevant endpoints related to that resource. For example, if a client goes to a resource's listing endpoint, that should include links to resources in that listing. And if there is pagination or limit being applied, it should have links to go to the rest of the items in the listing.

If a client has created a new resource, the new resource's link should be included in response as well which can be used for read, update, and delete operations on that resource by using different HTTP verbs. For operations other than typical CRUD, it will obviously have more URLs, so URLs for those operations should also be in the response, so that all endpoints related to the resource can be discoverable from one entry point.

Due to HATEOAS, an endpoint exposes links to related endpoints. This reduces the need of a thorough API documentation, although not completely, but one does not need to see the API documentation for the links already being exposed.

Code on demand (optional)

This states that the server can add more functionality to the REST client, by sending code that can be executable by that client. In the context of the web, one such example is JavaScript code that the server sends to the browser.

Let's consider an example to understand this better.

For example, a web browser acts like a REST client and the server passes HTML content that the browser renders. At the server side, there is some sort of server-side language which is performing some logical work at the server side. But if we want to add some logic which will work in the browser then we (as server-side developers) will have to send some JavaScript code to the client side and the browser and then execute that JavaScript code. So that the JavaScript code can add validation to a form, some animation or anything else, that couldn't be possible simply in HTML content. That JavaScript code is code on demand which the server sends to the client that extends the functionality of the REST client.

Note that sending code on demand to the client is optional, and not required if we don't want to extend the client's functionality.

Layered system

This constraint states that the REST system can have multiple layers and if a client is requesting for a response and getting a response, it can't be differentiated if it was returned from the server or another middle-ware server. So if one server layer is replaced by another, it doesn't affect the client unless it provides what it is expected to provide. In short, one layer doesn't have knowledge beyond the next layer with which it is interacting directly.

RESTful web services

As we have already defined REST and web services, we can now say that a RESTful web service is any web service that is REST-compliant.

Now, as we have already defined RESTful web services, we need to learn how RESTful web services work, and what RESTful web services are based on and why they are preferred over other web services such as SOAP.

Conventions of RESTful web services

RESTful web services are based on RESTful resources. A RESTful resource is an entity/resource that is mostly stored on a server and that client request using RESTful web services. Here are a few characteristics of a resource in terms of RESTful web services:

- It is an entity normally referred as a noun in the URL
- It is unique
- It has data associated with it
- It has at least one URI

If you are still wondering what exactly is a resource, consider the example of a blog. In a blog system, a **Post**, **User**, **Category**, or **Comment** can be a resource. In a shopping cart, a **Product**, **Category**, or an **Order** can be a resource. In fact, any entity which a client is requesting from the server is a resource.

Most commonly, there are five typical operations which can be performed on a resource:

- List
- Create
- Read
- Update
- Delete

For each operation, we need two things: the URI and HTTP method or verb.

The URI contains a resource name that is a noun and the HTTP method that is a verb. To perform some operation on an entity, we need to have a noun that tells us which entity we need to perform some operation. We also need to specify a verb to tell us what operation we want to perform.

For the preceding mentioned operations, there is a URL convention that we use with HTTP verbs and resource names. In the next section, we will review the URL structure and HTTP verbs for each operation.

HTTP verbs and URL structure

Here is how these operations can be performed on a resource using a combination of URIs and HTTP verbs. Note, in the following mentioned operation's URIs, you need to replace {resource} with a resource name.

List operation

- **HTTP method :** GET
- **URI:** /{resource}
- **Result:** It returns the list of the type of resource whose name is mentioned. In that list, it will give unique identifiers for the resource and these identifiers can be used to perform other operations on that particular resource.

Create operation

- **HTTP method :** POST
- **URI:** /{resource}
- **Parameters:** can be multiple parameters in POST body
- **Result:** This should create a new resource with parameters in the body.
- As you can see, there is no difference in the URI for Create and List but these two operations are distinguished by the HTTP method which results in different operations. In fact, a combination of the HTTP method and URI tells which operation should be performed.

READ operation

HTTP method: GET

URI: /{resource}/{resource_id}

Result: This should return the record based on the resource's ID.

Here resource_id will be the ID of the resource which can be found from the List operation's result.

Update operation

There can be two types of update operations:

- Update some attributes of a particular record
- Replace that particular record completely with a new one

Only thing that change to perform these two operations: HTTP method.

With the Update operation, to update some of attributes of the resource use:

HTTP method: PATCH

While to replace the whole resource use:

HTTP method: PUT

The URI and the parameters will remain the same:

URI: /{resource}/{resource_id}

Parameters: There can be multiple parameters in a query string. Initially, people try to pass these parameters in the body but actually, the PATCH and PUT parameters are passed using a query string.

Result: This should update or replace the resource based on the HTTP method.

Here, resource_id will be the ID of the resource which can be found from the List operation's result. Again, practically using PATCH or PUT will not make any difference but based on REST standards PATCH should be used for updating the different attributes of a record while PUT should be used for replacing the whole resource.

Delete operation

- **HTTP method**: DELETE
- **URI**: /{resource}/{resource_id}
- **Result**: This should delete the resource based on the resource ID in the URI

If you feel overwhelmed at the moment, don't worry, because right now we have just seen which combination of HTTP method and URI is used for which operations. Shortly, we will discuss a case study and will see some operations on different resources along with examples.

Before anything else, since we now know about RESTful web services and how they work, it's a good time to understand why we prefer to use RESTful web services over other web services.

Why RESTful web services?

In fact, RESTful web services are not the only type of web services that we can write. There are other ways to write web services as well. There are old ways of writing web services as well as some more recent ways. We will not go in to detail about other web services, as that is out of the scope of the book, with the focus here being on RESTful web services and how to build them.

REST versus SOAP

One old alternative to REST is SOAP. In fact, SOAP was already, used when REST came along as an alternative. A key difference is that SOAP doesn't have some particular convention that tells consumers how to access that. SOAP exposes its services using WSDL. Consider WSDL as a definition of services that SOAP provides. This is how the consumer knows what SOAP based web service provides and how to consume them.

On the other hand, REST emphasizes on "*conventions over configurations*". If you look at the URL structures and HTTP verbs of RESTful web services as we did earlier, there is a fixed convention. For example, if you are at the client side and want to create a product, if you know what parameters it will take then you can simply create it by sending a `POST` request to `example.com/product` and the resource will be created. If you want to list all the products, you can use the same URL with a `GET` request. If you get product IDs from the List operation, you can simply use them to update or delete a product by using `example.com/product/{product_id}` using `PATCH` and `PUT` or `DELETE` respectively. It is that simple to know what URL and HTTP method to use to do a type of operation because these are some conventions that RESTful web services follow. So, the one on the client end will just follow those conventions and will not need large documentations for simple tasks.

Other than that, simplicity of statelessness, separation of concerns, and cache-ability are some of the other advantages of RESTful web services that we have already seen in detail.

Nature of HTTP methods

Since we will be mainly dealing with URLs over HTTP and will be using HTTP methods, it is better to spend some time understanding the nature of HTTP methods.

We should also understand that HTTP methods are not actually doing any type of listing or creation or modification by themselves. It is just a convention to use certain HTTP methods and URL patterns for certain operations. These methods do not perform any operations on their own but it depends on the server-side developer. These methods can result in any operation depending on the code that the developer writes.

When we talk about the nature of HTTP methods, then it is about the convention and standards which are followed. After all, RESTful web services are about preferring convention over configuration. The foundation of today's HTTP and REST lies on these conventions and while writing RESTful web services, we are going to follow these conventions.

Safe/unsafe HTTP methods

HTTP methods can be both safe or unsafe. By safe, it means the methods are not expected to change any resource on the server and by unsafe it means the methods are expected to change some resource on the server. So this way, we have GET as the only safe method, as it is not expected to change anything on the server while other methods such as PUT, POST, PATCH, and DELETE are considered as unsafe methods since they are expected to do some changes on the server.

Idempotent and non-idempotent methods

There are methods which achieve the same results no matter how many time we repeat the same operations. We consider GET, PUT, PATCH, and DELETE as idempotent methods, as no matter how many times we repeat these method calls, it will always result in the same thing. For example, if you are using GET example.com/books, it will always return the same list of books, no matter how many times you call this URL with the GET method. However, if user put something else in database then it can have different result in listing but to declare some method idempotent or not, we are not considering change in result because of external factors instead of that method call itself. In the same way, if you use PUT or PATCH, let's say PATCH example.com/books/2?author=Ali, it will always result in the same response no matter how many times you call this method with the same parameters.

The same is the case with DELETE. It doesn't matter how many times you call DELETE on the same resource, it will only be deleted once. However, for DELETE, it can vary based on the implementation as well. It is something that depends on how you as a programmer want to implement. You probably want to DELETE and give a successful response the first time and on subsequent calls. You can simply give 404 because the resource no longer exists.

POST is non-idempotent because it creates a new resource on the server and the response has at least one unique attribute (mostly that is the ID of the resource), even if all the other attributes are same in the case of the same request parameters.

Until now, we have understood RESTful web services conventions, URL patterns, HTTP methods, and the nature of HTTP methods. However, it was mostly about requests. The URL and HTTP method are both request-related points. We haven't yet looked at responses, so now let's take a look into that.

HTTP response

The purpose of the request is to get a response or else it is of no use, considering that we also need to understand what type of response is expected against a request. There are two things that we will discuss in this context:

- Response type
- Response code

Response type

In the current world, many people think that the response of a RESTful web service must be a JSON or text having a JSON string. However, we can also use XML in response to a RESTful web service request. A lot of people use JSON in response because it is lightweight and easy to parse. But at the same time, this is just a matter of preference, and depends on the requirement and has nothing to do with REST standards.

Both XML and JSON are ways to format data. XML stands for Extensible Markup Language, having markup syntax. While JSON stands for JavaScript Object Notation, with JavaScript object-like syntax. For more understanding of JSON, please check out http://www.json.org/

We will shortly look into the case study of a blog and will see request and response examples. In this book, will use JSON as the response type, as JSON is simpler than XML. And while developing new applications, we mostly use JSON because it is lightweight and easy to understand. As you can see in the following examples, the same data in JSON is much simpler than XML and only has content that matters.

Here, we are trying to show the data of books having one or more authors:

XML:

```
<books>
  <book>
    <name>Learning Neo4J</name>
    <authors>
      <author>Rik Van Bruggen</author>
    </authors>
  </book>
  <book>
    <name>
     Kali Linux - Assuring Security by Penetration Testing
    </name>
```

```
    <authors>
      <author>Lee Allen</author>
      <author>Tedi Heriyanto</author>
      <author>Shakeel Ali</author>
    </authors>
  </book>
</books>
```

Now, let's look at the same example in JSON:

```
{
books: [
  {
    name:"Learning Neo4J",
    authors:["Rik Van Bruggen"]
  },
  {
    name:"Kali Linux - Assuring Security by Penetration Testing",
    authors:["Lee Allen", "Tedi Heriyanto", "Shakeel Ali"]
  }
  ]
}
```

You can clearly see from the preceding example, that XML and JSON both convey the same information. However, in JSON it is much easier as well as it needs a lot less words to show the same information.

Hence in the rest of book, we will be using JSON as the response type of our RESTful web services.

Response codes

Response codes, better known as HTTP status codes, tell us about the status of a request. If an HTTP request is successful, the HTTP status code is 200 which means OK. If there is a server error, it returns 500 status code which means an internal server error. In case of any problem in the request, the HTTP status code is 400 and onwards where 400 status code means a bad request. In case of redirection, the response code is 300 and onwards.

To see the complete list of response code and their usage, see `https://en.wikipedia.org/wiki/List_of_HTTP_status_codes`

I won't go into details of it as it would be redundant since all of it is already available at the preceding mentioned Wikipedia link. However, we will discuss the different status codes as we proceed.

Case study - RESTful web service endpoints for a blog

To understand RESTful web services, let's consider the case study of a blog where we will discuss resources/entities in a blog. We will start to define the requirements and endpoints URLs for the blog's resources and then define responses that we should have against those requests. So these endpoints and response definitions will help us understand how RESTful web services endpoint should look like and what the response should be. In the later chapters, we will talk more about the implementation of these endpoints, so these definitions will act as an API document for the next chapters. However, for simplicity, we will keep it minimal for now and later add more attributes to it.

Although based on HATEOAS, a RESTful web service should return links to the next endpoints and there are conventions that tell us about other endpoints but the API document is still important. API consumers (client-side developers) and API providers (server-side developers) should agree on it so that both can work in parallel without waiting for the other. However, in the real world, we don't have to write API document for basic CRUD operations.

In a typical blog, the most common resources are posts and comments. There are others as well but for now, we will discuss these two resources for the sake of understanding RESTful web services. Note that we are not considering authentication related stuff but will look into that in the later chapters.

If client-side and server-side teams are of the same organization, working on a single app, then it is a good idea to get such document created by the client-side team as the server-side team is just the serving client side.

Blog post

Here, we are listing the requirement of a blog post and its endpoints. For those endpoints, we will write a request and a response.

Requirements

A blog post can be created, modified, visited, and deleted. There should also be a way to list all the blog posts. So we are going to list the blog post's endpoints.

Endpoints

Here are the endpoints for blog post:

Creating blog post

- **Request**: `POST /posts HTTP/1.1`
- **Body parameters**:

    Content: This is an awesome post
    Title: Awesome Post

- **Response**:

```
{id:1, title:"Awesome Post", content:"This is an awesome post", link:
"/posts/1" }
```

- **Response code**: 201 Created

Here `POST` is the method, `/posts` is the URL (path after the server name) and HTTP 1.1 is the protocol. We will keep using the same way of mentioning requests in later examples as well. So, the first part of the request is the HTTP method, the second one is the URL and the third part is the protocol.

The response code tells the client that the resource has been created successfully. If a request parameter is missed by mistake, the response code should be **400**, which represents a bad request.

Reading blog post

- **Request**: `GET /posts/1 HTTP/1.1`
- **Response**:

    ```
    {id:1, title:"Awesome Post", content:"This is an awesome post",
    link: "/posts/1" }
    ```

- **Response code**: 200 OK

Note, if a blog post with an ID provided (in the current case, 1) does not exist, it should return **404**, which means resource Not Found.

Updating blog post

- **Request**: `PATCH /posts/1?title=Modified%20Post HTTP/1.1`
- **Response**:

```
{id:1, title:"Modified Post", content:"This is an awesome post",
link:"posts/1" }
```

- **Response code**: 200 OK

Note, if a blog post with the ID provided (that is 1 in this case) does not exist, it should return the response code **404** that means resource not found.

Also, we have used PATCH instead of PUT for the update since PATCH is used to modify all or some attributes of a record while PUT is used for modifying a whole record just like replacing an old record with a new one. So, if we use PUT and pass only one attribute, the other attributes will become empty. In the case of PATCH, it will only update the attribute that is passed and other attributes remain untouched.

Delete blog post

- **Request**: `DELETE /posts/1 HTTP/1.1`
- **Response**:

```
{success:"True", deleted_id:1 }
```

- **Response code**: `200 OK`

Note, if a blog post with an ID provided (in the current case, 1) does not exist, it should return **404**, which means resource `Not Found`.

Listing all blog posts

- **Request**: `GET /posts HTTP/1.1`
- **Response**:

```
{
data:[
  {
    id:1, title:"Awesome Post", content:"This is an awesome post",
```

```
link: "/posts/1"
  },
  {
    id:2, title:"Amazing one", content:"This is an amazing post",
link: "/posts/2"
  }
  ],
total_count: 2,
limit:10,
pagination: {
    first_page: "/posts?page=1",
    last_page: "/posts?page=1",
    page=1
  }
}
```

- **Response code:** `200 OK`

Here, data is an array of objects as there are multiple records returning. Other than `total_count`, there is a pagination object as well, and right now it shows the first and last pages because `total_count` for records is only 2. So, there is no next or previous page. Otherwise, we should also have to show the next and previous in pagination.

As you can see, there are links in the pagination as well as the post's links in post objects. We have included these links in response to being compliant with the HATEOAS constraint, which stated that if the client knows about an entry point, it should be enough to discover relevant endpoints.

Here, we explored the requirements of blog posts and defined the request and response of their endpoints. In the next entity/resource, we are going to define endpoints and responses in comments.

Blog post comments

Here, we are listing the requirements of a blog post comment and then its endpoints. For those endpoints, we will write `Request` and `Response`.

Requirements

There will be one, more than one, or no comments on posts. So, a comment can be created on a blog post. A blog post's comments can be listed. A comment can be read, modified, or deleted.

Let's define endpoints for these requirements.

Endpoints

Here are the endpoints for the post's comments:

Creating the post's comment

- **Request:** `POST /posts/1/comments HTTP/1.1`
- **Body parameters:** `comment: An Awesome Post`
- **Response:**

  `{id:1, post_id:1, comment:"An Awesome Post", link: "/comments/1"}`

- **Response code:** `201 Created`

Here in the case of a comment, a comment is created against a certain blog post. So, the request URL includes `post_id` as well.

Reading a comment

- **Request:** `GET /posts/1/comment/1 HTTP/1.1` or `GET /comment/1 HTTP/1.1`

  The second one seems more reasonable as in that one only needs to have a comment's ID without worrying about the post ID of that comment. And since a comment's ID is unique, we don't need to have the post's ID to get the comment. So, we will proceed with the second URL that is `GET /comment/1 HTTP/1.1`.

- **Response:**

  `{id:1, post_id:1, comment:"An Awesome Post", link: "/comments/1"}`

- **Response code:** `200 OK`

Since any comment can only exist against some post, the response includes `post_id` as well.

Updating a comment

- **Request:** `PATCH /comment/1?comment="Modified%20Awesome%20Comment' HTTP/1.1`
- **Response:**

  ```
  {id:1, post_id:1, comment:"Modified Awesome Comment", link:
  "/comments/1"}
  ```

- **Response code:** `200 OK`

Here, we used PATCH as we want to update a single attribute of a comment that is a comment. Also, you can see `%20` passed in a new comment. So, `%20` is just a replacement for a space as a URL cannot contain spaces. So with URL encoding, spaces should always be replaced by `%20`.

Deleting a post comment

- **Request:** `DELETE /comments/1 HTTP/1.1`
- **Response:**

  ```
  {success:"True", deleted_id:1 }
  ```

- **Response code:** `200 OK`

Note, if a post comment with an ID provided (in the current case, 1) does not exist, it should return **404 Not Found**.

Listing all comments for a particular post

- **Request:** `GET /posts/1/comments HTTP/1.1`
- **Response:**

  ```
  {
  data:[
    {
     id:1, comment:"Awesome Post", post_id:1, link: "/comments/1"
    }, {
     id:2, comment:"Another post comment", post_id:1, link:
  "/comments/2"
    }
   ],
  ```

```
total_count: 2,
limit: 10,
pagination: {
first_page: "/posts/1/comments?page=1",
last_page: "/posts/1/comments?page=1",
page=1
}
}
```

- **Response Code:** 200 OK

As you can see, a post's comments listing is very similar to a blog post's listing. And it has total_count and pagination in the same way. It shows the first and last page right now because total_count for the records is only 2. So there is no next or previous page. Otherwise, we should also have to show the next and previous links in pagination.

Normally, you don't see pagination with comments on blogs, but it is better to keep it consistent to have pagination in the listing. Because there can be lot of comments for a post, we should apply some limit to it, so we will need pagination.

More resources

Although we have tried to look into RESTful web services in a way that one gets practical knowledge with the examples, here are some other interesting resources.

Dissertation of Roy Fielding in which he introduced REST:

http://www.ics.uci.edu/~fielding/pubs/dissertation/top.htm

A group discussion with Roy Fielding's response:

https://groups.yahoo.com/neo/groups/rest-discuss/conversations/topics/6735

This is an interesting thread at stackoverflow.com regarding REST versus SOAP:

http://stackoverflow.com/questions/19884295/soap-vs-rest-differences

Roy Fielding talking about REST :

https://www.youtube.com/watch?v=w5j2KwzzB-0

A different way to look at REST:

https://www.youtube.com/watch?v=RY_kMXEJZfk

Summary

In this chapter, we understood what a RESTful web service is. We looked at constraints that should be fulfilled to be called as a RESTful web service. Then we understood that REST is an architecture and it is a way to build stuff and it favors convention over configuration. We looked at HTTP verbs (methods) and looked at URL conventions. We understood that these are just conventions. HTTP verbs and URLs are used in RESTful web services; otherwise it is always up to the developer to provide the expected behavior as REST has conventions which are just considered as standard but it don't provide any implementation.

In this chapter, we didn't talk about the implementation of RESTful web services. We just considered a case study of a typical blog and took examples of two resources of the blog and defined their endpoints with the expected responses. We also looked at HTTP response code but we didn't write actual code to implement these RESTful web services. We defined these endpoints, so we will see their implementation in the next chapters.

As this book is about building RESTful web services in the PHP7, in next chapter we will look at the features that came in PHP7. PHP7 does not offer anything specific to RESTful web services but we will be utilizing some of the new features in PHP7 to write better and clean code to build RESTful web services.

If you already know PHP7 well and don't wish to dig into that at the moment, you can skip Chapter 2, *PHP7, To Code It Better*, and start Chapter 3, *Creating RESTful Endpoints*, where we will build RESTful web services.

2
PHP7, To Code It Better

PHP7 came with many new features and changes. However, none of them were specifically for REST or web services. In fact, REST does not have any direct relation with language constructs. This is because REST is an architecture, while a language is there to provide constructs for implementation. So, does that mean PHP7 has some construct or feature which can make this implementation better? Yes and no. It depends on what we mean by implementation.

If we mean just getting a request and returning a response then No, there is no such specific feature. But, any RESTful Web Service is related to an entity, and an entity can have its own logic. So to provide RESTful Web Service for that entity, we need to write that logic as well. For this purpose, we will need to write more PHP code than just getting a request and returning a response. So to keep the code simple and clean, yes, PHP7 offers us many things.

I assume that you have the basic knowledge of PHP, as knowing PHP basics is a prerequisite of this book. So, we will not be looking at PHP5. In this chapter, we will be looking at many of the PHP7 features and changes, are either very important to know or we will be using in our code. We are directly going into these features. We are not going in to the details of installing or upgrading to PHP7 because there are dozens of tutorials available for that on the internet. Here is a list of features and changes we are going to discuss:

- Scalar type declaration
- Return type declaration
- Null coalescing operator
- Spaceship operator
- Group use statement
- Generator-related new features
    - Generator return expression
    - Generator delegation

- Anonymous classes
- `Closure::call()` function
- Errors and exceptions
- PHP7.1 features
  - Nullable types
  - Symmetric array destructuring
  - Support for keys in `list()`
  - Multi-catch exception handling

Scalar type declaration

In PHP7, we can now declare the type of parameters being passed to a function. They could be only user defined classes in previous versions, but now they can be scalar types as well. By scalar type, we mean basic primitive types, such as `int`, `string`, and `float`.

Previously, to validate an argument passed to a function, we needed to use some sort of `if-else`. So, we used to do something like this:

```php
<?php
function add($num1, $num2){
    if (!is_int($num1)){
        throw new Exception("$num1 is not an integer");
    }
    if (!is_int($num2)){
        throw new Exception("$num2 is not an integer");
    }

    return ($num1+$num2);
}

echo add(2,4);   // 6
echo add(1.5,4); //Fatal error:  Uncaught Exception: 1.5 is not an integer
```

Here we used `if` to make sure that the type of the variables $num1 and $num2 is int, otherwise we are throwing an exception. If you are a PHP developer from the earlier days who likes to write as little code as possible, then chances are that you were not even checking the type of parameter. However, if you do not check the parameter type then this can result in a runtime error. So to avoid this, one should check the parameter type and that is what PHP7 has made easier.

This is how we validate parameter type now in PHP7:

```php
<?php
function add(int $num1,int $num2){
    return ($num1+$num2);
}
echo add(2,4); //6
echo add("2",4); //6
echo add("something",4);
//Fatal error:  Uncaught TypeError: Argument 1 passed to add() must be of
the type integer, string given
```

As you can see now, we simply type hint as int and we do not need to validate each parameter separately. If an argument will not be an integer, it should throw an exception. However, you can see that it didn't show TypeError when 2 was passed as a string and instead it did an implicit conversion and assumed it as int 2. It did so because, by default, the PHP code was running in coercive mode. If strict mode is enabled, writing "2" instead of 2 will cause TypeError instead of the implicit conversion. To enable a strict mode, we need to use the declare function at the start of the PHP code.

This is how we can do this:

```php
<?php
declare(strict_types=1);

function add(int $num1,int $num2){
    return ($num1+$num2);
}

echo add(2,4); //6
echo add("2",4); //Fatal error:  Uncaught TypeError: Argument 1 passed to
add() must be of the type integer, string given,

echo add("something",4); // Fatal error:  Uncaught TypeError: Argument 1
passed to add() must be of the type integer, string given
```

Return type declaration

Just like parameter type, there is also a return type; it is also optional but it is a safe practice to specify the return type.

This is how we can declare a return type:

```php
<?php
function add($num1, $num2):int{
    return ($num1+$num2);
}

echo add(2,4); //6
echo add(2.5,4); //6
```

As you can see in the case of 2.5 and 4, it should be 6.5, but as we have specified int as a return type, it is performing implicit type conversion. To avoid this and to obtain an error instead of an implicit conversion, we can simply enable a strict type, as follows:

```php
<?php
declare(strict_types=1);
function add($num1, $num2):int{
    return ($num1+$num2);
}

echo add(2,4); //6
echo add(2.5,4); //Fatal error:  Uncaught TypeError: Return value of add()
must be of the type integer, float returned
```

Null coalescing operator

The Null coalescing operator (??) is a syntactical sugar, but a very important one. Previously in PHP5 when we were having some variable which could be undefined, we used the ternary operator as follows:

```php
$username = isset($_GET['username']) ? $_GET['username'] : '';
```

However, now in PHP7, we can simply write:

```php
$username = $_GET['username'] ?? '';
```

Although this is just a syntactical sugar, it can save time and make code cleaner.

Spaceship operator

The spaceship operator is also a shortcut for comparison and is very useful in user defined sorting functions. I am not going into detail about this, as it is already explained enough in its documentation: `http://php.net/manual/en/migration70.new-features.` `php#migration70.new-features.spaceship-op.`

Group use declarations

Classes, functions, and constants, which are in the same namespace, can be now imported in a single `use` statement. Previously, multiple `use` statements were required for that. Here is an example to understand it better:

```php
<?php
// use statement in Pre-PHP7 code
use abc\namespace\ClassA;
use abc\namespace\ClassB;
use abc\namespace\ClassC as C;

use function abc\namespace\funcA;
use function abc\namespace\funcB;
use function abc\namespace\funcC;

use const abc\namespace\ConstA;
use const abc\namespace\ConstB;
use const abc\namespace\ConstC;

// PHP 7+ code
use abc\namespace\{ClassA, ClassB, ClassC as C};
use function abc\namespace\{funcA, funcB, funcC};
use const abc\namespace\{ConstA, ConstB, ConstC};
```

As you can see from this example, how convenient the group use statement is, it is clearly visible. Curly braces with comma separated values are used to group values such as `{classA, classB, classC as C}`, resulting in the grouped `use` statement, instead of separately using the `use` statement for all these three classes, three times.

Generator-related features

Although generators came in PHP5.5, most PHP developers don't use them and most probably do not know about generators. So, let's first discuss generators.

What are generators?

As stated in the PHP manual:

> *Generators provide an easy way to implement simple iterators without the overhead or complexity of implementing a class that implements the iterator interface.*

OK, here is a more detailed and easy-to-understand definition from the same source, php.net:

> *A generator allows you to write code that uses foreach to iterate over a set of data without needing to build an array in memory, which may cause you to exceed a memory limit, or require a considerable amount of processing time to generate. Instead, you can write a generator function, which is the same as a normal function, except that instead of returning once, a generator can yield as many times as it needs to in order to provide the values to be iterated over.*

For example, you can simply write a function returning a lot of different numbers or values. But, the problem is that if a lot of different values means millions of values, then making and returning an array with those values is not efficient, because it will consume a lot of memory. So in that case, using generator makes more sense.

To understand, see this example:

```
/* function to return generator */
function getValues($max){
    for($i=0; $i<$max; $i++ ){
        yield $i*2;
    }
}

// Using generator
foreach(getValues(99999) as $value){
    echo "Values: $value <br>";
}
```

As you can see, there is a yield statement in code. It is just like the return statement but in generator, yield does not return all the values at once. It only returns a value every time yield executes, and yield is called only when the generator function is called. Also, every time yield executes, it resumes the code execution from where it was stopped the last time.

Now we have an understanding of generators, so let's look into the PHP7 features related to generators.

Generator return expression

As we have seen earlier, on calling a generator function, it returns a value that is being returned by the yield expression. Before PHP7, it didn't have the `return` keyword returning a value. But since PHP7.0, it is possible to use the return expression as well. Here, I have used an example from the PHP documentation, as it explains it very well:

```php
<?php

$gen = (function () {
    yield "First Yield";
    yield "Second Yield";

    return "return Value";
})();

foreach ($gen as $val) {
    echo $val, PHP_EOL;
}

echo $gen->getReturn(), PHP_EOL;
```

It will give the output as:

```
First Yield
Second Yield
return Value
```

So it clearly shows that calling a generator function in `foreach` will not return the `return` statement. Instead, it will just return at every yield. To get the `return Value`, this syntax: `$gen->getReturn()` can be used.

Generator delegation

As functions can call each other, similarly a generator can also delegate to another generator. Here is how a generator delegates:

```php
<?php
function gen()
{
    yield "yield 1 from gen1";
    yield "yield 2 from gen1";
    yield from gen2();
}
```

```php
function gen2()
{
    yield "yield 1 from gen2";
    yield "yield 2 from gen2";
}

foreach (gen() as $val)
{
    echo $val, PHP_EOL;
}


/* above will result in output:
yield 1 from gen1
yield 2 from gen1
yield 1 from gen2
yield 2 from gen2
*/
```

Here, `gen2()` is another generator being called in `gen()`, so a third yield in `gen()`, that is `yield from gen2();`, will transfer control to `gen2()`. So with that, it will start using yield from `gen2()`.

Note that `yield from` is only usable with arrays, traversable, or generators. Using another function (not generator) in `yield from` will result in a fatal error.
You can just consider it to be similar to how we can call a function in another function.

Anonymous classes

Just like anonymous functions, now there are anonymous classes in PHP. Note that if an object is required, then most probably we need some specific type of object and not just a random one, for example:

```php
<?php
class App
{
    public function __construct()
    {
        //some code here
    }
}
```

```php
function useApp(App $app)
{
    //use app somewhere
}

$app = new App();
useApp($app);
```

Note that a specific type of object was required in the useApp() function, and this type App couldn't be defined if it wasn't a class. So, where and why would we use an anonymous class with some specific functionality in it? We may need it in case we need to pass a class implementing some specific interface or extending some parent class, but only want to have this class used in one place. In that case, we can use an anonymous class.

Here is the same example given in the PHP7 documentation so that it will be easy for you to follow up:

```php
<?php
interface Logger {
    public function log(string $msg);
}

class Application {
    private $logger;

    public function getLogger(): Logger {
        return $this->logger;
    }

    public function setLogger(Logger $logger) {
        $this->logger = $logger;
    }
}

$app = new Application;
$app->setLogger(new class implements Logger {
    public function log(string $msg) {
        echo $msg;
    }
});

var_dump($app->getLogger()); //object(class@anonymous)#2 (0) {}
```

As you can see, although an anonymous class object is passed here in $app->setLogger(), it could be a named class object as well. So, an anonymous class object can be replaced by a named class object. However, it is better to use an anonymous class object when we don't want to use the object of the same class again.

Closure::call()

Binding an object scope with a closure is an efficient way to use a closure with different objects. At the same time, it is also a simple way to use different closures having different behaviors for an object in different places. This is because it binds the object scope with a closure at runtime without inheritance, composition, and so on.

However, previously we didn't have the `Closure::call()` method; we had something like this:

```php
<?php
// Pre PHP 7 code
class Point{
    private $x = 1;
    private $y = 2;
}

$getXFn = function() {return $this->x;};
$getX = $getXFn->bindTo(new Point, 'Point');//intermediate closure
echo $getX(); // will output 1
```

But now with `Closure::call()`, the same code can be written as follows:

```php
<?php
//  PHP 7+ code
class Point{
    private $x = 1;
    private $y = 2;
}

// PHP 7+ code
$getX = function() {return $this->x;};
echo $getX->call(new Point); // outputs 1 as doing same thing
```

Both code snippets perform the same action. However, PHP7+ code is shorthand. In case you need to pass some parameter to closure functions, you can pass it after objects as follows:

```php
<?php
// PHP 7+ closure call with parameter and binding

class Point{
 private $x = 1;
 private $y = 2;
}

$getX = function($margin) {return $this->x + $margin;};
echo $getX->call(new Point, 2); //outputs 3 by ($margin + $this->x)
```

Errors and exceptions

In PHP7, most errors are now reported as error exceptions. Only a few fatal errors halt script execution; otherwise, if you are carrying out error or exception handling, it will not halt the script. This is because now the Errors class implements a Throwable interface just like the Exception class, which also implements Throwable. So now, in most cases, fatal errors can be avoided through exception handling.

Here are some sub-classes of the error class:

- TypeError
- ParseError
- ArithmeticError
    - DivisionByZeroError
- AssertionError

This is how you can simply catch an error and handle it:

```
try {
    fn();
} catch(Throwable $error){
    echo $error->getMessage(); //Call to undefined function fn()
}
```

Here, $error->getMessage() is a method that is actually returning this message as a string. In our preceding example, the message will be similar to this: Call to undefined function fn().

This is not the only method you can use. Here is a list of methods that are defined in the Throwable interface; you can use them accordingly during error/exception handling. After all, the Exception and Error classes both implement the same Throwable interface:

```
interface Throwable
{
    public function getMessage(): string;
    public function getCode(): int;
    public function getFile(): string;
    public function getLine(): int;
    public function getTrace(): array;
    public function getTraceAsString(): string;
    public function getPrevious(): Throwable;
    public function __toString(): string;
}
```

PHP7.1

Till now, the preceding features that we discussed were PHP7.0 related. However, the recent version of PHP7 is PHP7.1, so it is worth discussing the important features of PHP7.1 as well, at least the features which we will use, or features that are worth knowing and using somewhere in our work.

In order to run the following code, you need to have PHP7.1 installed so, to do this, you can use the following commands:

```
sudo add-apt-repository ppa:ondrej/php

sudo apt-get update

(optional) sudo apt-get remove php7.0

sudo apt-get install php7.1 (from comments)
```

Remember that this is not an official upgrade path. The PPA is well-known, and is relatively safe to use.

Nullable types

If we are type hinting data types of parameters or return types of function, then it is important that there should be a way to pass or return the NULL data type instead of type mentioning as parameter or return type.

There can be different scenarios when we may need this, but always what we need to do is place a ? before the data type. Let's say we want to type hint string; if we want to make it nullable, that is to allow NULL as well, we will just type hint it as the ? string.

For example:

```php
<?php

function testReturn(): ?string
{
    return 'testing';
}

var_dump(testReturn());
// string(10) "testing"

function testReturn2(): ?string
{
    return null;
```

```
}

var_dump(testReturn2());
//NULL

function test(?string $name)
{
    var_dump($name);
}

test('testing');
//string(10) "testing"

test(null);
//NULL

test();
// Fatal error:  Uncaught ArgumentCountError: Too few arguments // to
function test(),
```

Symmetric array destructuring

It is not a big feature, but it is handy shorthand for list(). So it can be quickly seen in the following example:

```php
<?php
$records = [
    [7, 'Haafiz'],
    [8, 'Ali'],
];

// list() style
list($firstId, $firstName) = $records[0];

// [] in PHP7.1 is having same result
[$firstId, $firstName] = $records[0];
```

Support for keys in list()

As you can see in the previous example, list() works with an array and assigns to variables in the same order. However, as per PHP7.1, list() now supports keys. As [] is shorthand for list(), [] also supports keys.

Here is an example for the preceding description:

```php
<?php
$records = [
    ["id" => 7, "name" => 'Haafiz'],
    ["id" => 8, "name" => 'Ali'],
];

// list() style
list("id" => $firstId, "name" => $firstName) = $records[0];

// [] style
["id" => $firstId, "name" => $firstName] = $records[0];
```

Here, the ID `$firstId` will have 7 and `$firstName` will have `Haafiz` after the preceding code execution, no matter if either `list()` style is used or `[]` style is used.

Multi-catch exception handling

This one is an interesting feature in PHP7.1. It was previously possible but was performed in multiple steps. Now, instead of just catching one exception at a time and handling that, there is a multi-catch exception handling facility available. The syntax can be seen here:

```php
<?php
try {
    // some code
} catch (FirstException | SecondException $e) {
    // handle first and second exceptions
}
```

As you can see here, there is a pipe sign separating these two exceptions. So, this pipe sign | separates multiple exceptions. Here there are just two exceptions in the example, but there can be more than that.

More resources

We discussed new features of PHP7 and PHP 7.1 (recent version of PHP7) that we either found very important to discuss or which we are going to use in the rest of the book. However, we didn't discuss PHP7 features completely. You can find the PHP7 features list on php.net: `http://php.net/manual/en/migration70.new-features.php`.
Here, you can find all the new features of PHP 7.1: `http://php.net/manual/en/migration71.new-features.php`.

Summary

In this chapter, we discussed important PHP7 features. Also, we covered new PHP7.1 features. This chapter covers the fundamentals which will be used in the rest of this book. Note that using PHP7 features is not necessary, but it helps us to write simplified code efficiently.

In the next chapter, we will start creating a RESTful API in PHP as we discussed in Chapter 1, *RESTful Web Services, Introduction and Motivation*, while utilizing some of the PHP7 features.

3
Creating RESTful Endpoints

So far, we have understood what a RESTful web services. We have also seen the new features in PHP7 which will make our code better and cleaner. Now, it is time to implement RESTful web services in PHP. So, this chapter is all about implementation.

We have seen an example of a blog having blog posts and comment endpoints. In this chapter, we will implement those endpoints. Here are the topics that we will cover:

- Creating REST API for a blog in PHP
    - Creating a database schema
        - Blog user/author table schema
        - Blog post table schema
        - Blog post comments schema
    - Creating REST API's endpoint
        - Code structure
        - Common components
        - Creating blog post endpoints
        - To do
- Visible flaws
    - Validation
    - Authentication
    - Proper 404 pages
- Summary

Creating a REST API for a blog in PHP

To create REST API or RESTful web service for a blog, we first need to have blog entities. As we will be storing blog entities in a database and fetching the data from a database, we first need to create a database schema for those entities.

Creating a database schema

We are going to create endpoints for two resources/entities, which are :

- Blog post
- Post comments

So, we will be creating a database schema for these two resources.

Here is how we will design a database schema for a blog having posts and comments. A post can have multiple comments and a comment always belongs to post. Here, we have SQL for the database schema. You will first need to create a database and you will need to run the following SQL to have posts and comments tables. If you haven't created the database, then create it now. You can create it via some DB UI tool, or you can run the following SQL query:

```
create DATABASE blog;
```

This will create a database with the name `blog`.

Before creating a blog posts table and a blog post comments table, we will need to create a *users* table which will store the post or comment author's information. So first, let's create a users table.

Blog user/author table schema

A users table can have the following fields:

- `id`: It will have type integer, which will be unique and will have auto-incremented values. `id` will be the primary key of the users table.

- `name`: It will have type VARCHAR with a length of 100 characters. In the case of VARCHAR 100, 100 characters is the limit. If the title in one entry will be less than 100 characters, let's say only 13 character's, then it will occupy 14 characters space. This is how VARCHAR works. It occupies one character more than the actual characters in the value.

- `email`: Email address will have type VARCHAR with a length of 50. And the email field will be unique.

- `password`: Password will have type VARCHAR with a length of 50. We will be having the password field because later, at some stage, we will make the user log in using the email and password.

There can be a lot more fields but for simplicity, we will only keep these fields for now.

SQL for users table

The following is the SQL for users table. Note, we are using MySQL as RDBMS in our example. There can be a slight change in the queries for other databases:

```
CREATE TABLE `blog`.`users` (
`id` INT NOT NULL AUTO_INCREMENT ,
`name` VARCHAR(100) NOT NULL ,
`email` VARCHAR(50) NOT NULL ,
`password` VARCHAR(50) NOT NULL ,
PRIMARY KEY (`id`),
UNIQUE `email_unique` (`email`))
ENGINE = InnoDB;
```

This query will create a posts table as described above. The only thing that we haven't discussed is the database engine. The last line of this query ENGINE = InnoDB sets the database engine for this table as InnoDB. Also, on line 1, `blog` represents the name of the database. If you have named the database anything else other than blog, replace it with your database name.

We are only going to write the API's endpoint for posts and comments and are not going to write the endpoints for users, so we will add data to the users table manually using SQL Insert Queries.

Here are the SQL Insert Queries to populate the `users` table:

```
INSERT INTO `users` (`id`, `name`, `email`, `password`)
 VALUES
(NULL, 'Haafiz', 'kaasib@gmail.com',
'$2y$10$ZGZkZmVyZXJlM2ZkZjM0Z.rUgJrCXgyCgUfAG1ds6ziWC8pgLiZ0m'),
(NULL, 'Ali', 'abc@email.com',
'$2y$10$ZGZkZmVyZXJlM2ZkZjM0Z.rUgJrCXgyCgUfAG1ds6ziWC8pgLiZ0m');
```

As we are inserting two records having the `name`, `email`, and `password`, we set `id` to `null`. Since it is auto-incremented, it will be set automatically. Also, you can see a long random string in both records. This random string is the password. We set the same password for both users. However, the user will not be entering this random string as the password. This random string is encrypted an version of the user's actual password. The user's password is `qwerty`. This password was encrypted using the following PHP code:

```
password_hash("qwerty", PASSWORD_DEFAULT,
['salt'=>'dfdferere3fdf34dfdfdsfdnuJ$er']);
/* returns $2y$10$ZGZkZmVyZXJlM2ZkZjM0Z.rUgJrCXgyCgUfAG1ds6ziWC8pgLiZ0m
*/
```

The `password_hash()` function is the PHP recommended function for encrypting passwords. The first parameter is a `password` string. The second parameter is an encryption algorithm. While, the third parameter is an options array where we set a random string as salt. You can add a different salt as well.

However, this salt needs to be fixed for encrypting passwords every time because this encryption is a one-way encryption. That means the passwords can't be decrypted. So every time you need to match passwords, you will always have to encrypt the user provided password and match it with the one in the database. In order to match the user provided password and the one in the database, we need to use the same password function with the same arguments.

We are not making the user login functionality now, however, we will do that later.

Blog post table schema

A blog post can have the following fields:

- `id` : It will have type integer. It will be unique and have auto-incremented values. `id` will be the primary key of the blog post.

- `title`: It will have type `varchar` with a length of 100 characters. In the case of `varchar` 100, 100 characters is the limit. If one post title will be less than 100 characters, let's say a post's title takes only 13 characters, then it will occupy 14 character's space. It is how `varchar` works. It occupies one character more than the actual characters in the field.

- `status`: Status will be either published or draft. We will use `enum` for it. It has two possible values, `published` and `draft`.

- `content`: Content will be the body of the post. We will use the `text` data type for the content.

- `user_id`: `user_id` will be of type integer. It will be a foreign key and will relate with the `id` in the users table. This user will be the author of the blog post.

For the sake of simplicity, we will have only these five fields. The `user_id` will contain the information of the user who is the author of the post.

Here is an SQL query for creating a posts table:

The following is the SQL for a posts table. Note, we are using MySQL as RDBMS in our example. There can be a slight change in the queries for other databases:

```
CREATE TABLE `blog`.`posts` (
 `id` INT NOT NULL AUTO_INCREMENT ,
 `title` VARCHAR(100) NOT NULL ,
 `status` ENUM('draft', 'published') NOT NULL DEFAULT 'draft' ,
 `content` TEXT NOT NULL ,
 `user_id` INT NOT NULL ,
 PRIMARY KEY (`id`), INDEX('user_id')
)
ENGINE = InnoDB;
```

This query will create a posts table as described earlier.

Now, we add foreign keys to restrict the `user_id` to have only values which are present in the users table. Here is how we will add that constraint:

```
ALTER TABLE `posts`
ADD CONSTRAINT `user_id_foreign` FOREIGN KEY (`user_id`) REFERENCES
`users`(`id`) ON DELETE RESTRICT ON UPDATE RESTRICT;
```

Blog post comments schema

A blog post comment can have the following fields:

- id: It will have type integer. It will be unique and will have auto-incremented values. id will be the primary key of the blog post.

- comment: It will have type varchar with a length of 250 characters.

- post_id: post_id will be of type integer. It will be the foreign key related to the id from the posts table.

- user_id: user_id will be of type integer, it will be the foreign key, and will relate with the id in the users table.

Here, user_id is the ID of the author/writer of the comment while post_id is the ID of the post on which the comment is made.

Here is an SQL query for creating a comments table:

```
CREATE TABLE `blog`.`comments` (
 `id` INT NOT NULL AUTO_INCREMENT ,
 `comment` VARCHAR(250) NOT NULL ,
 `post_id` INT NOT NULL ,
 `user_id` INT NOT NULL ,
 PRIMARY KEY (`id`), INDEX(`post_id`), INDEX(`user_id`)
) ENGINE = InnoDB;
```

Adding foreign key constraints for both user_id and post_id:

```
ALTER TABLE `comments` ADD CONSTRAINT `post_id_comment_foreign` FOREIGN KEY
(`post_id`) REFERENCES `posts`(`id`) ON DELETE RESTRICT ON UPDATE RESTRICT;

ALTER TABLE `comments` ADD CONSTRAINT `user_id_comment_foreign` FOREIGN KEY
(`user_id`) REFERENCES `users`(`id`) ON DELETE RESTRICT ON UPDATE RESTRICT;
```

By running all these SQL queries, you will have most of the DB structure set up to proceed toward creating the RESTful API's endpoint in PHP.

Creating a RESTful API's endpoint

Before creating the RESTful API's endpoint specific to resources, let's first create directories in which we will place our code. Create a `blog` directory somewhere, your `home` directory, in case Linux is preferable. Then, create an `api` directory in the `blog` directory. We will place all our code in the `api` directory. If you are a command line fan or a seasoned Ubuntu user, simply run the following command to create these directories:

```
$ mkdir ~/blog //create blog directory
$ cd ~/blog //chang directory to blog directory
$ mkdir api //create api directory inside blog directory ~/blog
$ cd api //change directory to api directory
```

So, `api` is the directory where we will place our code. As you know, we are going to write code for endpoints related to two resources: blog posts and post comments. Before proceeding toward writing code specific to blog posts, let's first see how we are going to structure our code.

Code structure

Code can be written in many ways. We can either create different files for posts and comments such as `posts.php` and `comments.php` and let the user access them from a URL; for example, the user can write: `http://localhost:8000/posts.php` which can execute code in `posts.php`. The same can also be done in `comments.php`.

This is a very simple way but it has two problems:

- The first problem is that `posts.php` and `comments.php` will have different code. This means, if we have to use the same code across these different files, we will need to either write or include all common things in both these two files. In fact, if there will be more resources, then we will need to create a different file for every resource and in every new file, we will need to include all that common code. Although there are only two resources right now, we also need to think for extensibility. So in this approach, we will need to have the same code in all the files. Even if we are just doing include or require, we will need to do so in all files. However, this can be solved or minimized by having the minimum files to include or require.

- The second problem is related to how it will look in the URL. In the URL, the fact file to be used is mentioned, so what if after having our endpoints done and the API is given to frontend developers, we need to change the file name on the server? The web service from the frontend application will not work unless we change the file name in the URL in the frontend application. This points toward an important issue about our request and how the things stored on the server. So that means our code will be tightly coupled. This shouldn't happen as we stated in the constraints of REST in `Chapter 1`, *RESTful Web Services, Introduction and Motivation*. This `.php` extension exposes not only that we are using PHP at server side, but also our file structure is exposed to everyone who knows the endpoint URL.

The solution to problem one can be the include and require statements. Although, require or include statements will still be required to be in all files, and if one include statement needs to be changed in one file, we will need to do it in all the files. So, not a good way but the first problem can be solved. However, the second problem is a bit more critical. Some of you who have used the `.htaccess` file of Apache for URL rewriting will probably be thinking that URL rewriting will solve the problem. Yes, it can solve the problem of tight coupling between the request URL and the files on the file system but it will work only if we are using Apache as a server.

However, with the passage of time, you will see more and more use cases and you will realize that this way is not very scalable. In this, we are not following some pattern except that we are including the same code in all resource files. Also, using `.htaccess` for URL rewriting may work but it is not recommended to use it as a complete router because it will have its own limitations.

So what is the solution of this? What if we can have a single entry point? What if all the requests will go through that same entry point and then route toward the appropriate code? That will be a better approach. The request will be related to the post or comment, it must go through the same single entry point, and at that entry point we can include whatever code we want. That entry point will then route the request toward the appropriate code. This will solve both problems. Also, things will be in a pattern, as the code for each resource will follow the same pattern. This pattern that we just discussed is also known as the front controller. You can read more about the front controller at wiki: `https://en.wikipedia.org/wiki/Front_controller`.

Now we know that we will be using the front controller pattern so for that, our entry point will be `index.php` file. So let's create `index.php` in the `api` directory. For now, let's put an echo statement so we can test and run and see at least `hello world` using the PHP built-in server. Later, we will add proper content in the `index.php` file. So, put this in `index.php` for now:

```php
<?php

echo "hello World through PHP built-in server";
```

To test it, you will need to run the PHP built-in server. Note, you don't need to have Apache or NGINX just to run PHP code. PHP has a built-in server and, although this is good for testing and the development environment, this is not recommended for production use. As we are in the development environment on our local machine, let's run it:

```
~/blog/api$ php -S localhost:8000
```

This will let you hit `http://localhost:8000` and will output `hello World` through the PHP built-in server. So now, we are ready to start writing actual code to have our RESTful endpoints working.

Common components

Before proceeding toward endpoints, let's first identify and tackle things that we will need in serving all endpoints. Here are those things:

- Error reporting settings
- Database connection
- Routing

Open `index.php`, remove the old hello world code and place this code in the `index.php` file:

```php
<?php

ini_set('display_errors', 1);
error_reporting(E_ALL);

require __DIR__."/../core/bootstrap.php";
```

On the first two lines, we are basically making sure that we can see errors if there are errors in our code. The actual magic is happening in the last statement where we are requiring `bootstrap.php`.

It is just another file that we are going to create in the ~/blog/core directory. In the blog directory, we are going to create a core directory as we will keep a part of the code that is relevant to the flow and pattern of our code execution in the core directory. It will be the code that is not relevant to the endpoints or logic of our API. This core code will be created once and we can use the same core across different applications.

So, let's create bootstrap.php in the blog/core directory. Here is what we will write in bootstrap.php:

```php
<?php

require __DIR__.'/DB.php';
require __DIR__.'/Router.php';
require __DIR__.'/../routes.php';
require __DIR__ .'/../config.php';

$router = new Router;
$router->setRoutes($routes);

$url = $_SERVER['REQUEST_URI'];
require __DIR__."/../api/".$router->direct($url);
```

Basically, this is going to load everything and execute. bootstrap.php is the structure of how our application will run. So let's dig into it.

The first statement requires a DB class from the same directory, that is the core directory. The DB class is also a core class and it will be responsible for DB related stuff. The second statement requires a router that will direct the URL to proper files. While the third requires routes telling which file to serve in case of which URL.

We will look into both the DB and Router classes one by one but let's first look at routes.php having routes specified. Note that routes.php is application specific so it's content will vary based on our application URLs.

Here is the content of blog/routes.php:

```php
<?php

$routes = [
    'posts' => 'posts.php',
    'comments' => 'comments.php'
];
```

You can see it is just populating a `$routes` array. Here, posts and comments are part of the URL that we are expecting and if the URL will have posts, it will serve the `posts.php` file, and it will serve `comments.php` if the URL will have comments in it.

The fourth requirement in `bootstrap.php` is having application configurations such as DB settings. Here is a sample content of `blog/config.php`:

```php
<?php
/**
 * Config File
 */
$db = [
    'host' => 'localhost',
    'username' => 'root',
    'password' => '786'
];
```

Now, let's look at the DB and Router classes one by one so we can understand what exactly is going on in `blog/core/bootstrap.php`.

DB class

Here is the code of the DB class in `blog/core/DB.php`:

```php
<?php

class DB {

    function connect($db)
    {
        try {
            $conn = new PDO("mysql:host={$db['host']};dbname=blog",
$db['username'], $db['password']);

            // set the PDO error mode to exception
            $conn->setAttribute(PDO::ATTR_ERRMODE, PDO::ERRMODE_EXCEPTION);

            return $conn;
        } catch (PDOException $exception) {
            exit($exception->getMessage());
        }
    }
}
```

This class is related to the database. Right now, we have a constructor that is actually connecting to the database using PDO and $db arrays defined in blog/config.php. However, we will add more in this class later.

You can see we are using a PDO object here: **PDO (PHP Data Objects)**. It is used to interact with databases and is a recommended one because it doesn't matter which database we want to use, we just need to change the connection string and the remaining will work fine. This string: "mysql:host=$host;dbname=blog" is the connection string. This code in DB.php will create a connection with the database and this connection will close with the end of the script. We used try catch here because it is good to use exception handling when anything from outside of our code is being triggered.

Till now, we have looked into the DB class, routes.php (routes associative array), and config.php (settings associative array). Now we need to look into the content of the Router class.

Router class

Here is an implementation of the Router class at blog/core/Router.php:

```php
<?php

class Router {

    private $routes = [];

    function setRoutes(Array $routes) {
        $this->routes = $routes;
    }

    function getFilename(string $url) {
        foreach($this->routes as $route => $file) {
            if(strpos($url, $route) !== false){
                return $file;
            }
        }
    }
}
```

Router has two methods, Router::setRoutes(Array $routes) and Router::getFilename(). setRoutes() is taking an array of routes and storing it. Then, the getFilename() method is responsible for deciding which file to serve against which URL. We are not comparing the whole URL but we are using strpos() that checks if the string in $route exists in $url and, if it exists, it returns the appropriate filename.

Code sync

To make sure we are on the same page, here is what should be in your `blog` directory:

- `blog`
    - `blog/config.php`
    - `blog/routes.php`
    - `blog/core`
        - `blog/core/DB.php`
        - `blog/core/Router.php`
        - `blog/core/bootstrap.php`
    - `blog/api`
        - `blog/api/index.php`
        - `blog/api/posts.php`

Note, `blog/api/posts.php` doesn't have any proper content till now, so you can keep anything that can be just viewed in the browser so you know that this content is coming from `posts.php`. Other than that, if you are missing anything, then compare it with the code provided to you with this `book.boostrap.php` review.

Anyway, you have seen the content of all files included in `bootstrap.php`, so now you can look back at the `bootstrap.php` code to understand things better. That content is placed again so you can see it:

```php
<?php

require __DIR__ . '/DB.php';
require __DIR__.'/Router.php';
require __DIR__.'/../routes.php';

$router = new Router;
$router->setRoutes($routes);

$url = $_SERVER['REQUEST_URI'];
require __DIR__."/../api/".$router->getFilename($url);
```

As you can see, this is just including the `config` and `routes` files and including `Router` and `DB` classes. Here, it is setting the routes coming in `$routes`, as written in `routes.php`. And then, based on the URL, it is getting the filename which will serve that URL and require that file. We are using `$_SERVER['REQUEST_URI']`; it is a super global variable having a URL path that is after the host name.

Till now, we are done with common code making application structure. Now if your `blog/api/posts.php` contains code like my `posts.php`:

```php
<?php

echo "Posts will come here";
```

On starting the PHP server by saying: `php -S localhost:8000` and then in the browser hitting: `http://localhost:8000/posts`, you should see: *Posts will come here*.

In case you are unable to run it, I would suggest to go back and check what you have missed. You can also use the code given to you with this book. In any case, it is important to have this code written and running successfully at this point because just reading is not enough, practice makes you better.

Creating blog post endpoints

Till now, we are done with most of the common code. So let's look at blog post endpoints. In blog post endpoints, the first one is the blog posts listing.

Blog posts listing endpoints:

- URI: `/api/posts`
- Method: `GET`

So, let's replace the previous code in `posts.php` with the proper code to serve posts. And to serve this, put the following code in the `posts.php` file:

```php
<?php

$url = $_SERVER['REQUEST_URI'];

// checking if slash is first character in route otherwise add it
if(strpos($url,"/") !== 0){
    $url = "/$url";
}

if($url == '/posts' && $_SERVER['REQUEST_METHOD'] == 'GET') {
    $posts = getAllPosts();
    echo json_encode($posts);
}

function getAllPosts() {
    return [
        [
```

```
            'id' => 1,
            'title' => 'First Post',
            'content' => 'It is all about PHP'
        ],
        [
            'id' => 2,
            'title' => 'Second Post',
            'content' => 'RESTful web services'
        ],
    ];
}
```

Here, we are checking if the method is GET and the URL is /posts, and we are getting data from a function named getAllPosts(). For the sake of simplicity, we are getting data from a hardcoded array instead of a database. However, we actually need to get the data from the database. Let's add the code to get the data from the database. Here is what it will look like:

```php
<?php

$url = $_SERVER['REQUEST_URI'];
// checking if slash is first character in route otherwise add it
if(strpos($url,"/") !== 0){
  $url = "/$url";
}

$dbInstance = new DB();
$dbConn = $dbInstance->connect($db);

if($url == '/posts' && $_SERVER['REQUEST_METHOD'] == 'GET') {
  $posts = getAllPosts($dbConn);
  echo json_encode($posts);
}

;;
function getAllPosts($db) {
  $statement = $db->prepare("SELECT * FROM posts");
  $statement->execute();
  $result = $statement->setFetchMode(PDO::FETCH_ASSOC);
  return $statement->fetchAll();
}
```

If you execute this code, you will get an empty array in JSON format, which is fine. An empty array is shown as there is no record in the posts table right now. Let's create and use the add post endpoint.

Blog post creation endpoint:

- URI: /api/posts
- Method: POST
- Parameters: title, status, content, user_id

Now, we are just making these endpoints work without user authentication so we are passing user_id by ourselves. So, it should be id from users table.

To have this working, we need to add in posts.php. Then new code is mentioned in bold:

```php
<?php

$url = $_SERVER['REQUEST_URI'];

// checking if slash is first character in route otherwise add it
if(strpos($url,"/") !== 0){
 $url = "/$url";
}

$dbInstance = new DB();
$dbConn = $dbInstance->connect($db);

if($url == '/posts' && $_SERVER['REQUEST_METHOD'] == 'GET') {
 $posts = getAllPosts($dbConn);
 echo json_encode($posts);
}

if($url == '/posts' && $_SERVER['REQUEST_METHOD'] == 'POST') {
 $input = $_POST;
 $postId = addPost($input, $dbConn);
 if($postId){
     $input['id'] = $postId;
     $input['link'] = "/posts/$postId";
 }

 echo json_encode($input);
}


function getAllPosts($db) {
 $statement = $db->prepare("SELECT * FROM posts");
 $statement->execute();
 $result = $statement->setFetchMode(PDO::FETCH_ASSOC);
 return $statement->fetchAll();
}
```

```php
function addPost($input, $db){
 $sql = "INSERT INTO posts
 (title, status, content, user_id)
 VALUES
 (:title, :status, :content, :user_id)";

 $statement = $db->prepare($sql);

 $statement->bindValue(':title', $input['title']);
 $statement->bindValue(':status', $input['status']);
 $statement->bindValue(':content', $input['content']);
 $statement->bindValue(':user_id', $input['user_id']);

 $statement->execute();

 return $db->lastInsertId();
}
```

As you can see, we have placed another check, so if the method will be POST then it will run the addPost() method. In the addPost() method, POST is being added. We have used the same PDO prepare and execute statements.

However, this time we have also used bindValue(). First, we add a static string in the INSERT statement with a colon, such as :title, :status, and then we use a bind statement to bind the variable with those static strings. So what is the purpose of doing this? The reason is that we can't trust user input. Directly adding user input inside an SQL query can result in SQL injection. So to avoid SQL injection, we can use the PDO::prepare() function with PDOStatement::bindValue(). In the prepare() function, we provide a string while bindValue() binds the user input with that string. So, this PDOStatement::bindValue() doesn't only replace those strings with input parameters but makes sure that SQL injection doesn't occur.

We have also used PDO::lastInsertId(). This is to return the auto-incremented id of the record that was just created.

In the addPost() method, we are using the bindValue() method repeatedly for different fields. If there will be more fields then we probably need to write it even more times repeatedly. To avoid that, we change the addPost() method code to:

```php
function addPost($input, $db){

    $sql = "INSERT INTO posts
            (title, status, content, user_id)
            VALUES
            (:title, :status, :content, :user_id)";
```

```
$statement = $db->prepare($sql);

bindAllValues($statement, $input);

$statement->execute();

return $db->lastInsertId();
}
```

You can see PDOStatement::bindValue() calls are replaced with one bindAllValues() function call which takes PDOStatement as the first parameter and user input as the second parameter. bindAllValues() is a custom function that we have written, so here is an implementation of the bindAllValues() method that we will write in the same posts.php file:

```
function bindAllValues($statement, $params){
    $allowedFields = ['title', 'status', 'content', 'user_id'];

    foreach($params as $param => $value){
        if(in_array($param, $allowedFields)){
            $statement->bindValue(':'.$param, $value);
        }
    }

    return $statement;
}
```

Since we have written it as a separate generic function, we can use it in multiple places. Also, no matter how many fields in the posts tables we have, we will not need to call the same PDOStatement::bindValue() method repeatedly in our code. We will just add more fields in the $allowedFields array and the bindValue() method will be called automatically.

In order to test a POST request, we can't simply hit a URL from the browser. For testing a POST request, we need to use some sort of REST client or create and submit a form with POST. REST client is a better, easier and simpler way.

REST client

One of the very popular REST clients is Postman. Postman is a Google Chrome app. If you are using Chrome, then you can install this app from here: https://chrome.google.com/webstore/detail/postman/fhbjgbiflinjbdggehcddcbncdddomop/related?hl=en.

Once you open **Postman**, you will be able to select the method as **POST** or any other method and, on selecting the **Body** tab, you will be able to set field names and values and then hit **Send**. Check the following screenshot of **Postman** having fields set and the responses. This will give you an idea about how **Postman** can be used for post requests:

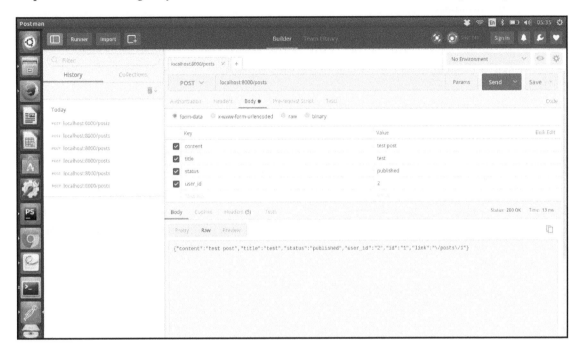

You can see the **POST** request has been sent through this **Postman** and it's result is successful as we intended. For all the endpoints testing, **Postman** can be used.

After running this **POST** based post creation endpoint, we can again test the listing of a post's endpoint and it will return data this time as now there is a post.

Let's look into get single post, update post, and delete post's endpoints.

Get single post endpoint:

- URI: `/api/posts/{id}`
- Method: `GET`

This URL with a `GET` method should return a single post based on the ID provided.

To make it happen, we need to do two things:

- Add a condition where the method is GET and the URL is of this pattern.
- We need to write and call the getPost() method that fetches a single post from the database.

We need to add the following code in posts.php.

First, we will add a condition and code to return single post:

```
if(preg_match("/posts\/([0-9])+/", $url, $matches) &&
$_SERVER['REQUEST_METHOD'] == 'GET'){
    $postId = $matches[1];
    $post = getPost($dbConn, $postId);

    echo json_encode($post);
}
```

Here, we are checking if the pattern is /posts/{id} where id can be any number. And then we are calling our custom function getPost() that will fetch the post record from the database. So, here is the getPost() implementation that we will add in the same posts.php file:

```
function getPost($db, $id) {
    $statement = $db->prepare("SELECT * FROM posts where id=:id");
    $statement->bindValue(':id', $id);
    $statement->execute();

    return $statement->fetch(PDO::FETCH_ASSOC);
}
```

This code is simply fetching a single record from the database as an associative array which can be clearly seen from the last line. Other than that, the SELECT query and its execution is simple enough.

Update post endpoint:

- URI: /api/posts/{id}
- Method: PATCH
- Parameters: title, status, content, user_id

Here {id} will be replaced by the actual post's ID. Note, as we are using the PATCH method, only those attributes should be updated that will be present in the input method.

 Here we are passing user_id as a parameter but it is just because we don't have authentication working otherwise it is strictly prohibited to pass user_id as parameter. user_id should be the id of authenticated user and that should be used instead of getting user_id in parameter. Because it can let any user pretend to be someone else by passing another user_id in parameter.

Please note that while using PUT or PATCH, parameters should be passed through a query string, only POST has parameters in the body.

Let's update our code of posts.php to support the update operation as well and we will then look more into that.

Here is the code to add in posts.php:

```
//Code to update post, if /posts/{id} and method is PATCH

if(preg_match("/posts\/([0-9])+/", $url, $matches) &&
$_SERVER['REQUEST_METHOD'] == 'PATCH'){
    $input = $_GET;
    $postId = $matches[1];
    updatePost($input, $dbConn, $postId);

    $post = getPost($dbConn, $postId);
    echo json_encode($post);
}

/**
 * Get fields as parameters to set in record
 *
 * @param $input
 * @return string
 */
function getParams($input) {
    $allowedFields = ['title', 'status', 'content', 'user_id'];

    $filterParams = [];
    foreach($input as $param => $value){
        if(in_array($param, $allowedFields)){
            $filterParams[] = "$param=:$param";
        }
    }
```

```
            return implode(", ", $filterParams);
    }



    /**
     * Update Post
     *
     * @param $input
     * @param $db
     * @param $postId
     * @return integer
     */
    function updatePost($input, $db, $postId){

        $fields = getParams($input);

        $sql = "
                UPDATE posts
                SET $fields
                WHERE id=':postId'
                 ";

        $statement = $db->prepare($sql);
        $statement->bindValue(':id', $id);
        bindAllValues($statement, $input);

        $statement->execute();

        return $postId;
    }
```

First, it checks if the URL is of the format : /posts/{id} and then checks if the Request method is PATCH. In that case, it calls the updatePost() method. The updatePost() method gets key value pairs as comma separated strings through the getParams() method. Then make a query, bind values, and postId. This is very similar to the INSERT method. And then in the condition block, we echo a JSON encoded form of the record that is updated. This is all very similar to what we did in the case of post creation and get single post.

One thing you should note is, we are getting parameters from $_GET that are query strings. It is because, in the case of PATCH and PUT, parameters are passed in query strings. So while testing through Postman or any other REST client, we need to pass parameters in query strings, not the body.

Delete post endpoint:

- URI: `/api/posts/{id}`
- Method: `DELETE`

This is very similar to getting a single blog post endpoint but here, the method is `DELETE`, so the record will be deleted instead of being viewed.

Here is the code to add in `posts.php` to delete a blog post record:

```
//if url is like /posts/{id} (id is integer) and method is DELETE

if(preg_match("/posts\/([0-9])+/", $url, $matches) &&
$_SERVER['REQUEST_METHOD'] == 'DELETE'){
    $postId = $matches[1];
    deletePost($dbConn, $postId);

    echo json_encode([
        'id'=> $postId,
        'deleted'=> 'true'
    ]);
}

/**
 * Delete Post record based on ID
 *
 * @param $db
 * @param $id
 */
function deletePost($db, $id) {
    $statement = $db->prepare("DELETE FROM posts where id=':id'");
    $statement->bindValue(':id', $id);
    $statement->execute();
}
```

After looking at insert, get, and update post's endpoint code, this code is very simple. Here, the main work is in the `deletePost()` method but it is also very similar to the other methods.

With that, we are now done with posts related to endpoints. However, right now all the data that we are returning as JSON it not actually JSON for client(browser or Postman). It is still viewing it as a string and considering it as HTML. It is because we are returning as JSON but it is still a string. To tell client to take it as JSON we need to specify `Content-Type` in header before any output.

```
header("Content-Type:application/json");
```

Just to make sure that our `posts.php` file is the same, here is a complete code of
`posts.php`:

```php
<?php

$url = $_SERVER['REQUEST_URI'];
if(strpos($url,"/") !== 0){
    $url = "/$url";
}
$urlArr = explode("/", $url);

$dbInstance = new DB();
$dbConn = $dbInstance->connect($db);


header("Content-Type:application/json");

if($url == '/posts' && $_SERVER['REQUEST_METHOD'] == 'GET') {
    $posts = getAllPosts($dbConn);
    echo json_encode($posts);
}

if($url == '/posts' && $_SERVER['REQUEST_METHOD'] == 'POST') {
    $input = $_POST;
    $postId = addPost($input, $dbConn);
    if($postId){
        $input['id'] = $postId;
        $input['link'] = "/posts/$postId";
    }

    echo json_encode($input);

}

if(preg_match("/posts\/([0-9])+/", $url, $matches) &&
$_SERVER['REQUEST_METHOD'] == 'PUT'){
    $input = $_GET;
    $postId = $matches[1];
    updatePost($input, $dbConn, $postId);

    $post = getPost($dbConn, $postId);
    echo json_encode($post);
}

if(preg_match("/posts\/([0-9])+/", $url, $matches) &&
$_SERVER['REQUEST_METHOD'] == 'GET'){
    $postId = $matches[1];
    $post = getPost($dbConn, $postId);
```

```
        echo json_encode($post);
    }

    if(preg_match("/posts\/([0-9])+/", $url, $matches) &&
    $_SERVER['REQUEST_METHOD'] == 'DELETE'){
        $postId = $matches[1];
        deletePost($dbConn, $postId);

        echo json_encode([
            'id'=> $postId,
            'deleted'=> 'true'
        ]);
    }

    /**
     * Get Post based on ID
     *
     * @param $db
     * @param $id
     *
     * @return Associative Array
     */
    function getPost($db, $id) {
        $statement = $db->prepare("SELECT * FROM posts where id=:id");
        $statement->bindValue(':id', $id);
        $statement->execute();

        return $statement->fetch(PDO::FETCH_ASSOC);
    }

    /**
     * Delete Post record based on ID
     *
     * @param $db
     * @param $id
     */
    function deletePost($db, $id) {
        $statement = $db->prepare("DELETE FROM posts where id=':id'");
        $statement->bindValue(':id', $id);
        $statement->execute();
    }

    /**
     * Get all posts
     *
     * @param $db
     * @return mixed
     */
```

```php
function getAllPosts($db) {
    $statement = $db->prepare("SELECT * FROM posts");
    $statement->execute();
    $statement->setFetchMode(PDO::FETCH_ASSOC);

    return $statement->fetchAll();
}

/**
 * Add post
 *
 * @param $input
 * @param $db
 * @return integer
 */
function addPost($input, $db){

    $sql = "INSERT INTO posts
            (title, status, content, user_id)
            VALUES
            (:title, :status, :content, :user_id)";

    $statement = $db->prepare($sql);

    bindAllValues($statement, $input);

    $statement->execute();

    return $db->lastInsertId();
}

/**
 * @param $statement
 * @param $params
 * @return PDOStatement
 */
function bindAllValues($statement, $params){
    $allowedFields = ['title', 'status', 'content', 'user_id'];

    foreach($params as $param => $value){
        if(in_array($param, $allowedFields)){
            $statement->bindValue(':'.$param, $value);
        }
    }

    return $statement;
}
```

```
/**
 * Get fields as parameters to set in record
 *
 * @param $input
 * @return string
 */
function getParams($input) {
    $allowedFields = ['title', 'status', 'content', 'user_id'];

    $filterParams = [];
    foreach($input as $param => $value){
        if(in_array($param, $allowedFields)){
            $filterParams[] = "$param=:$param";
        }
    }

    return implode(", ", $filterParams);
}


/**
 * Update Post
 *
 * @param $input
 * @param $db
 * @param $postId
 * @return integer
 */
function updatePost($input, $db, $postId){

    $fields = getParams($input);
    $input['postId'] = $postId;

    $sql = "
            UPDATE posts
            SET $fields
            WHERE id=':postId'
            ";

    $statement = $db->prepare($sql);

    bindAllValues($statement, $input);

    $statement->execute();

    return $postId;

}
```

Note, this code is very basic and it has many flaws that we will see in the next chapters. This is just to give you a direction of how you can do it in core PHP but this is not the best approach.

To do

As we are done with Post CRUD endpoints, you need to create the Comments CRUD endpoints. It shouldn't be difficult as we have already put comments in routes by which you know that we will add `comments.php` similar to `posts.php`. And you can also view the logic in the `posts.php` file, as `comments.php` will have same operations and will have the similar code. So now, it is your time to code for `comments.php` CRUD related endpoints.

Visible flaws

Although the code we discussed in the previous sections will work, there are many loopholes in it. We will look into the different problems in the next chapters, however here let's see three of them here and also see how we can solve them:

- Validation
- Authentication
- No response in case of 404

Validation

Right now in our code, although we are using `PDO` prepare and `bindValue()` methods, it will just save it from SQL injection. However, we are not validating all fields in the case of insert and update. We need to validate that the title should be of a specific limit, the status should be either draft or published, and the `user_id` should be always one of IDs in the users table.

Solution

The first and simple solution is to place manual checks to validate data coming from the user's end. This is simple but it is a lot of work. That means it will work but we can miss something, and if we do not miss any check, it will be a lot of low level detail to deal with.

So a better way is to utilize some open source package or tool already available in the community. We will look and use such tools or packages in the upcoming chapters. We will also use such packages to validate data in the upcoming chapters.

In fact, this is not only true about validation, but there is still a lot of low level work that we are doing by ourselves in this chapter. So, we will look at how we can minimize our efforts on low level stuff by using different tools available in the PHP community.

Authentication

Right now, we are letting anyone add, read, update, and delete any record. It is because there is no authenticated user. Once there is an authenticated user, we can place different constraints such as that a user shouldn't be able to delete or update the content of a different user and so on.

So why didn't we simply put in place session based authentication having a **Session ID** in an HTTP Only cookie? This is done in traditional websites. We start the session, put the user data in session variables and the session ID is stored in an HTTPOnly cookie. The server always reads that HTTP Only cookie and gets a session ID to know which session data belongs to this user. This is what happens in a typical website developed in PHP. So why don't we simply use the same thing for authentication in the case of RESTful web services?

Because RESTful web services are not intended to be only called through a web browser. It can be anything such as a mobile device, another server, or it can be a **SPA (Single Page Application)**. So, we need a way that can work with any of these things.

Solution

A solution is that we will use a simple token, instead of a session ID. And instead of cookies, that token will be just sent to the client and the client will always take that token in every request to identify the client. Once the client is taking the token in every request, it doesn't matter if the client is a mobile application, SPA, or anything else. We will simply identify the user based on the token.

Now the question is how to create and send back a token? This can be done manually but again, why create it if this is already available in open source and tested by the community? In fact, in the later chapters, we will use such a package, and use tokens for authentication.

Proper 404 pages

Now we don't have a proper 404 page if the page or record we are looking for doesn't exist. It is because we are not handling this in our router. The router is very basic but again, this is low level stuff and we can find such routers in open source. We will use this in later chapters as well.

Summary

We created a basic RESTful web service and provided basic CRUD operations. However, there are a lot of issues in the current code which we will see and address in the next chapters.

We have written PHP code to create a basic RESTful web service in this chapter, though it is not the best way to do it--this is just to give you a direction. Here are some resources from where you can learn to write better PHP code. This is a quick reference for PHP best practices: http://www.phptherightway.com/.

To adopt the standard coding style and practice, you can read PHP coding standards and style at http://www.php-fig.org/.

I recommend that you spend some time on these two URLs so that you can write better code.

In the next chapter, we will look into this in detail and will identify different flaws in this code including security and design flaws. And also, look at different solutions.

4
Reviewing Design Flaws and Security Threats

In this chapter, we will review our work, the endpoints we implemented, and will look into two different aspects in which our current work can be improved and should be improved. We will also look at:

- Our code structure and design flaws
- Security threats and how we can mitigate them

Then, we will look at ways to move forward to implement a RESTful API with the improvements discussed in the preceding two sections.

Finding problems in the current code

Till now, we have written our blog post's endpoint-related code, and I left you to do the same with the comment-related endpoints. If you haven't done that, then I insist that you do that first, or at least try to do so because without practice, it doesn't last for much time, so keep practicing at least when some code examples are provided or there are some tasks to do.

Anyway, as we have written code to implement RESTful web service endpoints in the last chapter, we are going to dig into that and identify what is missing and what types of improvements are required.

Structural and design flaws

Right now in our code, there are some flaws that we can identify very clearly.

Missing query builder layer

Although we are using PDO, we still always need to write a query and need to carry out many low level things such as being aware of SQL injection (due to which we have to use the prepare statement, then bind values), to perform database-related operations. We should use some sort of query builder layer, which can make queries for us. So once we have that layer, we don't need to write SQL queries again and again.

Although PDO makes it easy to swap one database connection with another, still there are some SQL queries which will need to be changed for different databases. In fact, it is not only good for changing the DBMS but also, having a sort of query builder is time saving because using query builder, we are not always dealing with strings to build queries as with query builder we can also use arrays or associative arrays to build queries.

Incomplete router

The router we implemented is just routing different files, such as /posts which was being served through posts.php. Our router did not specify which function of posts.php will serve that request. We were specifying this from inside posts.php, based on the URL pattern. Just to remind you, here is that conditional portion of posts.php:

```php
if($url == '/posts' && $_SERVER['REQUEST_METHOD'] == 'GET') {
    $posts = getAllPosts($dbConn);
    echo json_encode($posts);
}
```

Doing that isn't difficult. We can simply put such conditions in router.php and call an appropriate function in posts.php. However, if you remember our routes.php file, it was a very simple file having key value pairs. Putting that here again for your ease:

```php
<?php

$routes = [
    'posts' => 'posts.php',
    'comments' => 'comments.php'
];
```

As you can see, we are not specifying the Request method anywhere in `routes.php`, so we will need to specify that in `routes.php` as well. Other than that, we will also need to use a regular expression in `routes.php` instead of a plain URL. Doing this is easy in `routes.php`, but the actual place where we will need to add implementation will be `core/router.php`. It can be done, but we will not do that. We don't make components such as routers from scratch, because it is not something that is being done for the first time in the world. So how do we do it? We can use a router from open source components or packages which are already available. Later on, we will see how we can reuse already present open source packages or components.

Usage of OOP

We should use an object-oriented paradigm as it is not only good to make code better and cleaner, but it also makes development faster with the passage of time because clean code reduces the friction in our way to code for more features or to modify code.

Separate Configurations from Implementation

Configurations should be better. It is good that we have a `config` file which has database connection information, but there are many other things which should be in configurations, for example, whether to show errors or not should be controlled through the `config` file.

So the rule of thumb is that we should separate configurations from implementations. This is important so that we can always change configurations without being worried about the implementation of code responsible for logic and so on.

Should write tests

No matter if you are writing a RESTful web service or making a website, writing test cases is always important. For that purpose, code must also be testable. So tests (unit tests) not only test the code against requirements, but also check if the code is flexible enough and loosely coupled. Tightly coupled code can not be that much testable as compared to loosely coupled code.

Writing test cases in code also makes code cleaner and more agile, which can be modified easily. In the case of a web service, API tests are also convenient.

Input validation

As stated in the last chapter, we didn't validate data coming from input sources although we avoided SQL injection as we were using the PDO `prepare()` and `bindValue()` methods. It was because we only wrote code in the last chapter to understand and learn. Otherwise, not having input validation is not only inconvenient but also insecure for applications.

To apply validation, we can either use manual checks or write a validator where we can simply pass input parameters and check against particular rules. This type of validator is very convenient, but writing a good validator also takes time, so it is better to use an already present open source validator. As you can see, we tried to write a router and then found issues. These issues could be fixed, but we would need to write more code and writing more code takes time.

In later chapters, we will see how we can use someone else's written validator, and we will use that to make RESTful web service endpoints. We are not only trying to save or time to write code but we are trying to avoid to have more code, whose maintenance will become our responsibility.

Handling 404 and other errors

Right now, we haven't handled 404 if there is a wrong URL or ID for a blog post or comment so we will need to deal with that, not only by sending the not found error, but also by sending the HTTP status code as 404. So for different responses, we will need to send different HTTP status codes.

Meta information missing

Right now, there is no record count, no pagination is there. All records are being shown there. So if there will be lot of records, let's say a few million records, then returning all records will not make sense. In that case, we should apply pagination and there should be a proper place in response where meta information should be shown.

DB fields abstraction

Right now, all data coming from the database is being shown to the user as it is. What if field names will change and the client side developer is using that DB field? It will start giving an error at the client side as well.

If you remember, one of the important constraints of REST is abstraction between what the server returns to the client and how a server actually stores data. So, we need to keep this abstraction. In upcoming chapters, we will see how we can keep that abstraction.

Security

As you can see, we haven't applied any type of security at all. In fact, we haven't made all endpoints login protected. But, it isn't possible in the real world to not have a login or authentication. So, we will need to make some endpoints login protected.

In this chapter, we are only going to see how we can implement security for our endpoints, but we will not implement that yet and will implement it in later chapters. Right now we are looking at how we will make some resources login protected, because based on that, we will be able to identify other security risks as well. So in the next section of this chapter, we are going to see how authentication will work.

Securing API endpoints

First, we need to understand how authentication and login works. The first time client side application sends login credentials (that is mostly email address and password). On the basis of those credentials, the server-side login endpoint makes the user's login and returns a token against that authenticated user. That token is stored on the client side. On every request, the client side has that token either in a request body or in a request header. It can be more clearly seen in the following diagram.

The first client will hit the login endpoint on the server with the login credentials:

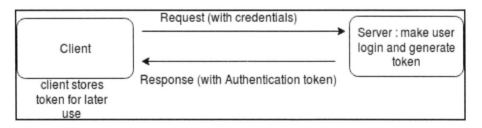

Once the client gets the token, the client will store it for later use. Then with every request, the client will send the same token so that the server can consider the client as authenticated:

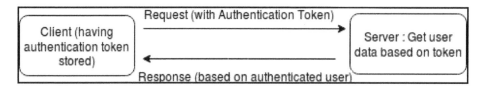

When a server will find the client authenticated, it will return data based on the authenticated user.

If there is no token sent with a request where only authenticated user is allowed then server should return 401 HTTP status code that is unauthenticated or unauthorized.

For example, consider **POST** endpoints. There are endpoints such as create post, modify post, and delete post; these need to be protected, so there should be an **Auth middleware** protecting these endpoints, while other endpoints such as show post and list posts and some other **GET**-based endpoints shouldn't be login protected, so **Auth middleware** should be there for protected endpoints. It is as follows:

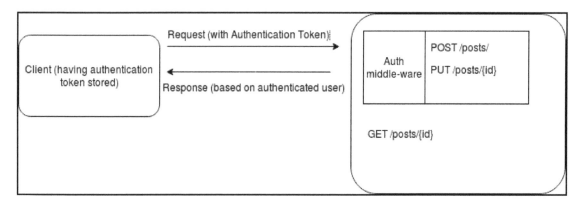

As you can see in this diagram, the server will respond based on the provided authentication token and **Auth middleware** is just there to resolve a user from the authentication token. However, if **Auth middleware** will not able to resolve a user from the authentication token, it will simply return a 401 unauthorized error.

What is Auth middleware?

Auth middleware will be nothing more than a piece of code that will validate an authentication token and will try to resolve the user against that authentication token. It will be just a piece of code that will be attached to some endpoints in the routes or place from where the data for the endpoint is being returned. In any case, it will execute before the actual code for the endpoint and will validate and resolve the user from the `auth` token in Request.

In `Chapter 6`, *Illuminating RESTful Web Services with Lumen*, we will look into middleware and in `Chapter 7`, *Improving RESTful Web Services*, we will write code for authentication middleware.

Common security threats in RESTful web services

Since we have looked at problems in our current code and how we will be implementing security in some of our endpoints and use authentication middleware, now it is the time to see what the common security threats that we need to consider while building RESTful web services are.

Use of HTTPS

HTTPS is HTTP with SSL. As our data is being transferred over the internet, we need to make our connection secure; for that reason, we should use HTTPS. The purpose of HTTPS is to make sure that the server is who it claims to be and that data is transferred between the client and server with a secure connection in an encrypted form.

If you don't want to buy an SSL certificate as it is costly for you, then you can simply go for `https://letsencrypt.org/`. Let's Encrypt is a free certificate authority. So, you can use it without paying for an SSL certificate.

Securing an API key/token

As our sessions will be based on a token, we need to secure that authentication token. There are different things that need to be done for that:

1. Not passing an access token in the URL.
2. Access token expiration.

Not passing an access token in the URL

The API key or token or whatever sensitive information needs to be sent to the server, should not be passed in the URL as this can be captured in web server logs. So, it must be passed in the POST body or Request Headers.

Access token expiration

An access token should be expired in two cases. First, it should be expired on logout. Second, the access token should expire after a fixed amount of time, and this duration shouldn't be long. The reason for expiring a token is that it is safer to have an access token valid for less time. If we have many access tokens which are not in use, then there are more chances that those tokens can be misused.

The expiration period can be around two hours or less. Although it depends on how you want to implement it, a shorter expiration period is more secure. Expiration does not mean that the user will need to log in again, instead there will be a token refresh endpoint. That will be hit with the last expired token against a particular user to get a new token. Please note that last token should be usable for refresh token endpoint till a limited time, after that last token shouldn't be usable to refresh token. Otherwise, what's the point in expiring a token. Remember that there are trade offs between both ways. Refresh token on every request is more secure but cause more overhead for server. So it is always up to you that which way you prefer in your scenario.

The other way to expire a token is not to expire it by time, but by refreshing a token on every request. For example, if a request is sent with one token, the server will validate that token, refresh the token, and send a new token in response. So the old token will not be usable. The token will be refreshed on every request. It can be done in both ways; it is up to you how you prefer it.

Limited scope access token

It is also a good idea to limit the scope of the access token to avoid problems if some one unauthorized has got the token. Also, if a service is being provided to a client-side application that is not specific to some user or access, then it should still have some sort of API key, by which we can identify who is asking for information. So, if there is a suspicious attempt to access an API endpoint with some API key, we can simply revoke the specific API key, so it will be no longer valid for future requests. It is only possible if there are multiple API keys having the limit access level.

Public and private endpoints

Just like public web pages, we can have public endpoints for RESTful web services as well. All endpoints that are available to the user before authentication are not public. Sometimes, we make endpoints which are open to use before login, or without login, but they are only intended to be accessible through our application. Those endpoints are not public, so we do not want those endpoints to be accessible through other applications. For that purpose, we will be using some sort of API key, as discussed earlier.

We can use an `oauth2`-based access token. A big advantage of using an `oauth2` access token is that if we are making different applications to access similar endpoints, then we can have different access tokens for different applications.

Example: We can have an online book store API exposed as a RESTful web service, and we can have two applications:

- Book selling `app`. For customers.
- Book selecting `app`. For teachers.

Now through a customer's `app`., users can browse different books and add to cart and buy. While in the teachers `app`., users can browse and select different books to forward to a person who will buy books later. These two different apps. will have some endpoints in common and some endpoints different to each other. But, we don't want any endpoint to be publicly available to everyone. So, we can have two different access levels and will make two different mobile `apps`. having two different API keys, each having different access levels. When a user logs in, we will return an access token with limited access. Different tokens can have different access levels based on the user role.

Let's say in the teacher `app.`, there can be some teachers who can only select books while some other teachers, let's say the **HOD** (**Head of Department**) can also buy books. So after login, both of these users can have a different access token translating into a different access level. This access level will be on the basis of the access token which will be translated into a user who is logged in, and we will get a role from the user on the basis of which we will decide the access level.

Public API endpoints

So even before login, these endpoints were private. What if we have some API endpoints that are public, such as a weather forecast giving forecast data to everyone. It is better to still have an API key to track who is getting data to the server, but what if this is not the case and we are just giving data without any API keys? Does that mean that we are giving that data publicly, so we don't need to worry about anything? Actually, no.

If a client is passing any information to the server, then it is better to have TLS that should be used to encrypt data. Other than that, we also can't allow anyone to keep hitting an endpoint; to make usage fair, we need to apply throttling, which means an API endpoint can be hit only a limited number of times in a specific period of time from one client.

Insecure direct object reference

Insecure direct object reference refers to getting or providing sensitive information based on data coming from Request. This is not a problem in only RESTful web services but also in websites. To understand that, let's consider an example:

Let's say we are going to change a user's first name or billing address. It is better to refer it to an endpoint such as: `PATCH /api/users/me?fist_name=Ali` (having token in header), rather than `PATCH /api/users/2?fist_name=Ali` (having token in header).

To let a user modify his/her own data, it will have a token in the header by which a server will make sure that this user can modify a record. But, which record? In the endpoint with `me`, it will just get a user based on the token and will modify its `first_name`.

While in the second case, we have the user's `id=2`, so the user can be fetched or updated based on the user `id=2`, which is not secure as the user can pass any user ID in the URL. So, the problem is not this type of URL, the problem is getting or updating the record based on the reference directly from user input or the request from a client. No matter what user ID is provided, if we intend to modify a logged in user's first name, then it should get or update the user based on token and not the user ID in the URL.

Restricting allowable verbs

We need to restrict allowable verbs. For example if a web service endpoint is only for read purpose and not for modification, then on the URL, `/api/post/3`, we should only allow `GET method/verb` but shouldn't allow `PATCH`. `PUT`, `DELETE`, or `POST`. If someone hits `/api/post/3` with `PATCH`, `PUT`, `DELETE`, or `POST`, it shouldn't serve it, instead it should return an "405 Method Not Allowed" error.

However, if their client has an access token and based on that, the user is only allowed to use the `GET` method (although there are other methods available) and not other methods, and the client with that user hits the same URL with other methods, then there should be an "403 Forbidden" error, because there are methods allowed but just not to the current user based on its role or permissions.

Input validation

It seems that input validation is probably not very related to technology, but it is very important to validate input because it is not only beneficial to have clean data in a database, but it is also useful to protect against different threats such as XSS and SQL injection.

Actually, XSS prevention and different input validation is an important part of input validation, while SQL injection is mainly prevented while entering data in a database. Another type of threat which needs to be prevented is CSRF, but that will already be prevented by the API key or authentication token usage. However, a separate CSRF token can also be used.

Available reusable code

We haven't discussed each and every security threat, but we used some things which needed to be taken care of to avoid security-related problems. We have discussed how we should secure our endpoints and how to implement authentication for RESTful web services. We also discussed flaws in our current code that we wrote in the previous chapter.

However, we haven't written code to make our code better and more secure. We can do this, but we should understand that there is already a lot of stuff to utilize instead of doing everything from scratch. So instead of writing everything in plain PHP by ourselves, we will use available code. It is not only to save time but also to use something that is available in the community and is time tested by the community.

So if we have made up our minds to use a third-party code snippet, package, or class, then we should understand that in PHP there is not one group of developers writing code in one framework. There are lots of PHP classes available as individual classes. Some are written for some frameworks. Some are written for Open Source CMS such as WordPress. There are also some packages available in **PEAR (PHP Extension and Application Repository)**. So code available in one place may not be useful or compatible with other code.

In fact, just loading different code snippets together could also be a problem, especially when there are a lot of dependencies.

So, here comes the revolution in the PHP community. It isn't a framework or CMS or open source class or extension. It is a dependency manager for PHP, known as Composer. We can install Composer packages in a standard way and Composer has been a standard for most of PHP's popular frameworks. We will not talk more about Composer here because Composer is the topic of the next chapter, so we will talk about it in detail as we will be using Composer a lot for package installations, dependency management, auto-loading, and more. Not only in this book but if you are going to make any proper application in PHP, you will need a composer. So the reusable code that we will use will be mostly through Composer packages.

Summary

We already have discussed problems and missing parts in our current code and security threats, and we have discussed how we will implement authentication. We also discussed that we will use reusable components or code to save our time and effort. Also, because the code will be written by ourselves, we will be responsible for its maintenance and testing, so using open source stuff which is not only available but in many cases is tested, as well as maintained by the community, makes more sense. For that purpose, we will be mostly using Composer as it has become a standard tool for packaging and using reusable packages in PHP.

In the next chapter, you will learn more about Composer. What it is, how it works, and how we can use it for different purposes.

 We have talked about security threats in this chapter, but we have not covered them in lots of detail because we only had one chapter to discuss them. But, web application and RESTful Web service security is a wide topic. There is a lot more to learn about it. I would recommend you to go and check `https://www.owasp.org/index.php/Category:OWASP_Top_Ten_Project` as a starting point. There is a lot of stuff you will learn from there and you will learn from a different perspective.

5
Load and Resolve with Composer, an Evolutionary

Composer is not only a package manager, but also a dependency manager in PHP. In PHP, if you want to reuse an open source component, the standard way to do it is to use an open source package through Composer, as Composer has become a standard for making packages, installing packages, and auto-loading. Here, we have discussed a few new terms, such as package manager, dependency manager, and auto-loading. In this chapter, we will go into detail of what they are and what Composer provides for them.

The preceding paragraph explains what Composer mainly does, but Composer is more than that.

In this chapter, we will look at the following things:

- Introduction to Composer
- Installation
- Usage of Composer
    - Composer as a package and dependency manager
    - Installing packages
        - How Composer works
        - Composer commands
        - The `composer.json` file
        - The `composer.lock` file
    - Composer as an autoloader

Introduction to Composer

The PHP community is a sort of divided one and there are lot of different frameworks and libraries. Since there are different frameworks available, a plugin or package written for one framework cannot be used in another. So, there should be a standard way to write and install packages. Here comes Composer. Composer is a standard way to write, distribute, and install packages. Composer is inspired by **npm** (**Node Package Manager**) from the node.js ecosystem.

In fact, most developers use Composer to install the different packages they use. This is also because using Composer to install a package is convenient because packages installed through Composer can also be easily auto-loaded through Composer. We will look into auto-loading later in this chapter.

As stated before, Composer is not just a package manager, but also a dependency manager. This means if a package needs something, Composer will install those dependencies for it and it will then auto-load accordingly.

Installation

Composer requires PHP 5.3.2+ to run. Here is how you can install Composer on different platforms.

Installation on Windows

On Windows, installing Composer is very easy, so we will not go into much detail. You just need to download and execute the Composer setup from getcomposer.org. Here is the link: https://getcomposer.org/Composer-Setup.exe.

Installation on Linux/Unix/OS X

There are two ways to install Composer, they are locally and globally. You can simply install Composer through the following commands:

```
$ php -r "copy('https://getcomposer.org/installer', 'Composer-setup.php');"
$ php -r "if (hash_file('SHA384', 'composer-setup.php') ===
'669656bab3166a7aff8a7506b8cb2d1c292f042046c5a994c43155c0be6190fa0355160742
ab2e1c88d40d5be660b410') { echo 'Installer verified'; } else { echo
'Installer corrupt'; unlink('composer-setup.php'); } echo PHP_EOL;"
```

```
$ php composer-setup.php
$ php -r "unlink('composer-setup.php');"
```

The preceding four commands perform the following tasks respectively:

1. Downloads the Composer setup PHP file
2. Verifies the Installer by checking SHA-384
3. Runs the Composer setup to install Composer
4. Removes the downloaded Composer setup file

If you are curious about what this Composer setup does, then leave the fourth command. As you can see, the setup file is a PHP file named `composer-setup.php`; you can simply open this file and read the code. What it mainly does is check several PHP extensions and settings and creates the `composer.phar` file. This `composer.phar` will be responsible for performing Composer tasks. We are going to look at what Composer does and what actions or tasks it performs in this chapter shortly.

Using the aforementioned commands, we have installed Composer locally. By default, it will install Composer in the current directory by installing Composer, which means by placement of the `composer.phar` file, because this `composer.phar` file performs Composer functionality.

If you wish to install Composer (placing `composer.phar`) in a specific directory or change the `composer.phar` name to something else, you can simply run the install with different parameters, such as:

```
php composer-setup.php --install-dir=bin --filename=composer
```

There are many other parameters, which you can see at `https://getcomposer.org/download/` under "Installer Options".

If you have installed Composer locally and the filename is `composer.phar`, you can simply run it through PHP by saying:

```
php composer.phar
```

This will run Composer. If `composer.phar` is not in the same directory as before `composer.phar`, you need to append the path of the directory where the `composer.phar` file is. This is because we have installed Composer locally. So, let's see how we can install it globally.

Global Installation

To install and access Composer globally from anywhere, we need to place it in a directory that is added in the system's PATH directory.

To do that, we can run the following command to move composer.phar to a place from where we can access it globally:

```
sudo mv composer.phar /usr/local/bin/Composer
```

Now you will simply be able to access Composer by running command, composer and it will work; nothing else will be required. So, if you say:

```
composer -V
```

It will return something like the following:

```
composer version 1.4.2 2017-05-17 08:17:52
```

You can run this command from anywhere, since we have Composer installed globally.

Usage of Composer

Composer is a dependency manager and has other different uses. Composer is used to install packages while resolving dependencies. Composer is also very good at auto-loading. There are more uses of Composer as well. Here, we will discuss the different uses of Composer.

Composer as a dependency manager

Composer is a dependency manager. Now you can package your code in a way that you don't need to ship third-party dependencies with it. You just need to tell its dependencies. In fact, your package dependencies can have more dependencies, and those dependencies can also have more dependencies. So, resolving all those dependencies while making a package or bundle could be really tiresome. But it is not, thanks to Composer.

Since Composer is also a dependency manager, dependencies are not a problem anymore. We can just specify dependencies in a JSON file, and those dependencies are resolved by Composer. We will look into that JSON file shortly.

Installing packages

If we have dependencies (other packages on which our work depends or is going to depend) in a JSON file named `composer.json`, then we can install them through Composer.

There are a lot of good packages in PHP and most of the stuff related to our daily work is available, so who would want to reinvent the wheel and create everything again? So, to start a project, we can simply install different packages through Composer and reuse a lot of code that is already there.

Now, the question is, what is the source from where Composer can be installed? Can it be anything anywhere on the internet? Or are there some fixed places from where Composer installs packages? Actually, there can be multiple sources. The one default place from where Composer installs a package is Packagist `https://packagist.org/`.

So, we are going to install a package from Packagist. Let's say we want to install a PHP unit testing framework package from Packagist. It is available here: `https://packagist.org/packages/phpunit/phpunit`.

So, let's install it with the following command:

```
composer require phpunit/phpunit
```

You will see that this package installation will also result in the installation of a lot of dependencies as well. Here, `require` is a Composer command, while `phpunit/phpunit` is the name with which this package is registered on Packagist. Note, we just discussed about a `composer.json` file but we didn't need the `composer.json` file, to install this PHP unit package. Actually, the `composer.json` file is useful if we already have some dependencies. If we just need to install some packages right now, then we can simply use the `composer require` command. And this `composer require` will also create a `composer.json` file and update it with the `phpunit/phpunit` package.

Here is the content of the `composer.json` file that will be created after running the preceding command:

```
{
    "require": {
        "phpunit/phpunit": "^6.2"
    }
}
```

You can see in the require object, it has the key of package name and then, after the colon, there is "^6.2", which represents the package version. Here, the package version is given in a regular expression stating that the package version is starting from 6.2, but this isn't the actual version that is installed. After packages and their dependencies are installed, their exact version is written in the composer.lock file. This file, composer.lock, has significant importance, so we will look into it in detail shortly.

After running this command, you will be able to see another directory in the directory where you ran the Composer require command. This other directory is the vendor directory. In the vendor directory, all packages are installed. If you look into it, not only is the PHP unit present in the vendor directory, but also all of its dependencies and dependencies of dependencies are installed in the vendor directory.

Installing using composer.json

Instead of using composer require, we can also install a package through another command if we have a composer.json file. To do so, go into another directory. We can simply make a composer.json file having a list of packages with the following content:

```
{
    "require": {
        "phpunit/phpunit": "^6.2",
        "phpspec/phpspec": "^3.2"

    }
}
```

So, once you have a file named composer.json and have this content in it, you can simply install these two packages with their dependencies based on this version information by running this command:

```
composer install
```

This will do the same thing that Composer require did. However, if both composer.json and composer.lock files are present, it will read information from the composer.lock file and will install that exact version and ignore composer.json.

If you want to ignore the composer.lock file and install based on information in the composer.json file, you can either delete the composer.lock file and use the composer install or you can run:

```
composer update
```

Note, the `composer update` command will also update the `composer.lock` file.

If a package or library isn't available on Packagist, you can still install that package through other sources, and to do so you will need to enter different information in the `composer.json` file. You can read detailed information about other sources here `https://getcomposer.org/doc/05-repositories.md`. However, note that Packagist is the recommended source because of its convenience.

The composer.json in detail

The `composer.json` file that we have seen is minimal. To see what a typical `composer.json` file looks like, here is the `composer.json` file of my favorite PHP MVC framework Laravel:

```json
{
    "name": "laravel/laravel",
    "description": "The Laravel Framework.",
    "keywords": ["framework", "laravel"],
    "license": "MIT",
    "type": "project",
    "require": {
        "php": ">=5.6.4",
        "laravel/framework": "5.4.*",
        "laravel/tinker": "~1.0"
    },
    "require-dev": {
        "fzaninotto/faker": "~1.4",
        "mockery/mockery": "0.9.*",
        "phpunit/phpunit": "~5.7"
    },
    "autoload": {
        "classmap": [
            "database"
        ],
        "psr-4": {
            "App\\": "app/"
        }
    },
    "autoload-dev": {
        "psr-4": {
            "Tests\\": "tests/"
        }
    },
    "scripts": {
        "post-root-package-install": [
```

```
            "php -r \"file_exists('.env') || copy('.env.example',
    '.env');\""
        ],
        "post-create-project-cmd": [
            "php artisan key:generate"
        ],
        "post-install-cmd": [
            "Illuminate\\Foundation\\ComposerScripts::postInstall",
            "php artisan optimize"
        ],
        "post-update-cmd": [
            "Illuminate\\Foundation\\ComposerScripts::postUpdate",
            "php artisan optimize"
        ]
    },
    "config": {
        "preferred-install": "dist",
        "sort-packages": true,
        "optimize-autoloader": true
    }
}
```

We will not go into obvious parts of this file, such as name, description, and so on. We will look into complex and more important attributes.

The require object

You have already seen that `require` has dependencies and version information which are installed by the `composer install` command.

The require-dev object

In `require-dev`, only those packages which are required during the development phase are listed. We used an example, of `phpunit/phpunit` in the Composer install example but actually, packages like `phpunit` and `phpspec` are only required in development and not in production. Also, if there are any packages required related to debugging, they can also be included in the `require-dev` object. And the `composer install` command will install all the packages which are in `require-dev`, as well as under `require` object.

However, if we want to only install packages which are required in production, they can be installed with:

```
composer install --no-dev
```

In the aforementioned example, `composer.json`, `laravel/tinker` and `laravel/laravel` are in the `require` object, but `phpunit`, `mockery`, and `faker` are the packages mentioned in the `require-dev` object, so those will not be installed.

The autoload and autoload-dev

This autoload option is there to autoload either a namespace or group of classes under one directory or simply a class. It is a PHP autoloader alternative that Composer provides. This is what tells Composer which directory to look into while auto-loading a class.

The auto-load property has two more properties, that is `classmap` and `psr-4`. PSR4 is a standard that describes specifications for auto-loading classes from file paths. You can read more about it at `http://www.php-fig.org/psr/psr-4/`.

Here, PSR-4 is specifying a namespace and from where this namespace should be loaded. Here, in preceding the example, the `App` namespace should be getting content from the `app` directory.

Another property is `classmap`. This is used to auto-load libraries which don't support PSR-4 or PSR-0. PSR-0 is another standard for auto-loading, however, PSR-4 is newer and is the recommended one. PSR-0 is already deprecated.

Just as `require-dev` is similar to `require`, `autoload-dev` is similar to `autoload`.

The scripts

Scripts basically have scripts in arrays against different events. All those properties of script objects are sort of events, and scripts specified in values executed at specific events. Different properties represent different events, such as `post-install-cmd` means after installing packages it will execute scripts in an array against the `post-install-cmd` property. It's the same with other events. On this URL in the Composer documentation, you can find details of all these events: `https://getcomposer.org/doc/articles/scripts.md#command-events`.

The composer.lock

The main purpose of `composer.lock` is to lock dependencies.

As discussed, the `composer.lock` file is very important. This is because when a specific exact version is not specified in `composer.json` or a package is installed through `composer require` without version information, Composer installs the package and, after installing, adds information regarding that package installation including the exact version (that is installed).

If, package is already in `composer.lock`, then most probably you have the package listed in `composer.json` as well. In that case, you normally install the package through `composer install` and Composer will read the package details and version information from `composer.lock` and install exactly that version because that is what Composer does, locking dependencies with the exact version.

If there is no `composer.lock` file in your code base, `composer install` or `composer require` will install package(s) which will create the `composer.lock` file as well.

If the `composer.lock` file is already there, then it will make sure that Composer install will install the exact version written in `composer.lock` file and it will ignore `composer.json`. However, as mentioned earlier, if you want to update your dependencies and want to update that in the `composer.lock` file, then you can run `composer update`. This is not recommended, because once your application is running on specific dependencies and you don't want to update, then the `composer.lock` file is useful. So, if you want to lock down dependencies, don't run the `composer update` command.

If you are working in a team, you must commit the `composer.lock` file as well, so that other team members in your team can have the exact same packages and versions. So, committing the `composer.lock` file is highly recommended and not a matter for discussion.

We are not going to discuss `composer.lock` in detail, as this is most of what we need to know about `composer.lock`. However, I would recommend you open and read `composer.lock` once. Understanding everything is not necessary, but it will give you some idea.

It basically has package information that is installed with the exact version that is installed and its dependencies.

Composer as an auto-loader

As you have seen, there is auto-loading related information available in the `composer.json` file because Composer is also responsible for auto-loading. In fact, even without that auto-load property specified, Composer can be used to auto-load files.

Previously, we were using `require` or `include` to load every file separately. You don't need to `require` or `include` each and every file separately. You just need to require or include one file, that is `./vendor/autoload.php`. This `vendor` directory is Composer's vendor directory, where all packages are placed. So, this `autoload.php` file will auto-load everything without worrying about including all files with their dependencies in order.

Example

Let's say we have a `composer.json` file like this:

```
{
  "name": "laravel/laravel",
  "description": "The Laravel Framework.",
  "keywords": [
    "framework",
    "laravel"
  ],
  "license": "MIT",
  "type": "project",
  "require": {
    "php": ">=5.6.4",
    "twilio/sdk": "5.9.1",
    "barryvdh/laravel-debugbar": "^2.3",
    "barryvdh/laravel-ide-helper": "^2.3",
    "cartalyst/sentinel": "2.0.*",
    "gocardless/gocardless-pro": "^1.0",
    "intervention/image": "^2.3",
    "laravel/framework": "5.3.*",
    "laravelcollective/html": "^5.3.0",
    "lodge/postcode-lookup": "dev-master",
    "nahid/talk": "^2.0",
    "predis/predis": "^1.1",
    "pusher/pusher-php-server": "^2.6",
    "thujohn/twitter": "^2.2",
    "vinkla/pusher": "^2.4"
  },
  "require-dev": {
    "fzaninotto/faker": "~1.4",
    "mockery/mockery": "0.9.*",
    "phpunit/phpunit": "~5.0",
    "symfony/css-selector": "3.1.*",
    "symfony/dom-crawler": "3.1.*"
  },
  "autoload": {
    "classmap": [
      "app/Models",
```

```
      "app/Traits"
    ],
    "psr-4": {
      "App\\": "app/"
    }
  },
  "autoload-dev": {
    "classmap": [
      "tests/TestCase.php"
    ]
  }
}
```

With that `composer.json` file, if we run `composer install`, it will install all these packages, then, to load all those packages and all the classes in:

```
      "app/Models",
      "app/Traits"
```

We will need to just include one file, like this:

```
require __DIR__.'/vendor/autoload.php';
```

And this will make all those packages available in your code. So, all these packages, and our own `classes/traits` within `app/Models` and `app/Traits`, will be available even though while we didn't include all those packages separately. So, Composer works as an auto-loader as well.

Composer for creating a project

We can also use Composer to create a new project from an existing package. This is equivalent to performing two steps:

- Cloning a repository
- Running `composer install` in that

That means it will clone a project and install its dependencies. It can be done with the following command:

```
composer create-project <package name> <path on file system> <version info>
```

It is very useful if we want to start a project from a code base. Note, the path on the filesystem and version number is not required, but optional.

Example

To install a framework named Laravel, you can simply run:

```
composer create-project laravel/laravel
```

Here, `laravel/laravel` is the package. As you can see from this, the path on the filesystem or version is not mentioned here. This is because those parameters are optional.

With those parameters, this command will look like this:

```
composer create-project laravel/laravel ./exampleproject 5.3
```

Summary

Composer is a standard way to make and use reusable components. Nowadays, a lot of stuff has already been done and can be reused. For this reason, in PHP, Composer is a standard method. In this chapter, we have seen how Composer works, what it's usages are, how can one install packages through it, and a lot more. However, one thing that we haven't touched on in this chapter is how we can make packages for Composer. This is because our focus was on how we can reuse already available Composer packages. If you want to learn how to a create Composer package, then start from here: `https://getcomposer.org/doc/02-libraries.md`.

If you want to know more about Composer, you can:

1. Go and read Composer documentation at `https://getcomposer.org/doc/`.
2. Open and start reading important files. You can open and read different Composer files, such as `composer.json` and `composer.lock`, from different packages.

Till now, we have seen how we can reuse Composer components to avoid writing everything on our own. In the next chapter, we will start using such components or projects to make our RESTful web service better.

6
Illuminating RESTful Web Services with Lumen

So far, we have created a very basic RESTful web service in Core PHP and identified flaws regarding design and security. We have also seen that to make things better we don't need to create everything from scratch. In fact, using open source code that is time tested makes more sense, to build better web services based on cleaner code.

In the last chapter, we have seen that Composer is a dependency manager for PHP projects. In this chapter, we will use an open source micro-framework to write RESTful web services. We will do the same work in an open source micro-framework that is in active development, time tested and well known in PHP community. The reason for using a framework instead of few components is that a proper framework can make a good structure of our code, and it comes with some basic required components. The micro-framework we have chosen is Lumen, a micro-framework version of the full-stack framework Laravel.

Here is what we intend to cover in this chapter:

- Introducing Lumen
    - What Lumen provides
    - What Lumen has in common with Laravel
    - How Lumen is different from Laravel
- Installation and configuration
- Database Migrations

- Writing REST API in Lumen
    - Routes
    - Controllers
    - REST Resource
    - Eloquent (Model)
        - Relationships
- User Access and Token based Authentication and Session
- API Versioning
- Rate Limits
- Database Seeders of Users
- Using Lumen Packages for REST API
- Reviewing Lumen based REST API
- Need of encryption
- Different SSL Options
- Summary and more resources

Introducing Lumen

Lumen is a micro-framework version of the full-stack framework Laravel. In the PHP community, Laravel is a very well-known framework. So by using Lumen, we can always convert our project to Laravel and start using its full-stack capabilities if we have to.

Why micro-framework?

Every thing has a cost. We chose a micro-framework instead of a full-stack framework, because although a full-stack framework provides more features, to have those features it has to load more stuff. So to provide the luxury of more features, a full-stack framework has to compromise a bit on performance as compared to a micro-framework. The micro-framework on the other hand, lets go of some features which are not required for building web services like views and so on, which makes it faster.

Why Lumen?

Lumen is not the only micro-framework in the PHP community. So why Lumen? There are three major reasons for that:

- Lumen is micro-framework of Laravel, so with a little effort we can always convert it into Laravel and utilize its full-stack capabilities.
- As Lumen is a micro-framework of Laravel, it has awesome community support just like Laravel. A good community is always a very important factor. At the same time, Lumen is able to use a lot of the same packages that Laravel uses.
- Other than its relation with Laravel, Lumen is also very good with respect to performance. Based on performance, other alternative micro-frameworks could be Slim and Selex.

What Lumen provides

As we know that Lumen is a micro-framework version of Laravel, it provides a lot of capabilities that Laravel provides. For example, it is an MVC framework. However, it is good to know what Lumen and Laravel have in common and what Lumen doesn't have or has different. This will give us a good idea of what Lumen has in store for us.

What Lumen has in common with Laravel

Here, I didn't say similarities between Laravel and Lumen, because Lumen is not a completely different framework. I said what is common in both of them, because they have common packages and components: that means they share the same code base in many cases.

Actually, Lumen is sort of a small, minimal Laravel. It just drops some of the components and uses different components for some tasks like routes. However, you can always turn on a lot of components in the same installation. Sometimes, you don't even need to write some code in the configuration for that. Instead, you just go to the configuration file and uncomment some lines of code and it starts using those components.

In fact, Lumen has the same versions. For example, if there is 5.4 version of Laravel, Lumen will have the same version. So, these are not two different things. They have most things similar to each other. Lumen just drops some unrequired stuff for the sake of performance. However, if you just want to convert your application code that is written for Lumen to Laravel, you can simply put that code in a Laravel installation and it should mostly work. No major change in your application code is needed.

How Lumen is different from Laravel

As Lumen is built for micro-services and APIs, components related to front-end like an elixir, authentication bootstrap, sessions and views and so on do not come with Lumen out of the box, but these can be included later on, if required: it is very flexible in that.

Routes are different in Lumen. In fact, it doesn't use Symfony router; instead it uses a different router which is faster but has fewer features. This is because Lumen sacrifices features for speed. Similarly, there are no separate configuration files like Laravel. Instead, some configurations are done in .env file while others related to registering a provider or alias and so on are done in the bootstrap/app.php file, probably to avoid loading different files for the sake of speed.

Both Lumen and Laravel have a lot of packages and a lot of them work for both. Still, there are packages which were mainly built for Laravel and don't work with Lumen without some changes. So if you intend to install a package, make sure it supports Lumen. For Laravel, most of the packages work for Laravel because Laravel is more popular and most of the packages were built for Laravel.

What exactly Lumen provides

You are probably thinking that this is the difference between Lumen and Laravel, but what exactly does Lumen provide us so we can build API? We will look into it, but not in detail, because Lumen documentation at https://lumen.laravel.com/docs/5.4 serves this purpose. What is not covered in the documentation is how we can make a RESTful web service using Lumen, and what packages we can utilize to make our work and life easier. We will look into this.

First, we will discuss what comes with Lumen, so that we understand its different components and working.

A Good Structure

Lumen comes with a good structure. As it is derived from Laravel, which follows the MVC (Model View Controller) pattern, Lumen also has a Model and Controller layer. It does not have the view layer, because it does not need views: it is for web services. If you don't know what MCV is, consider it just an architectural pattern where responsibilities are distributed in three layers. Model is a DB layer and sometimes also used as business logic layer (we will look into what should be in the model in a later chapter). The view layer is for template related stuff. Controller can be considered a layer handling requests while getting data from Model and rendering View. In case of Lumen, there are only Model and Controller layers.

Lumen provides us a good structure so we don't need to make it on our own. In fact, Laravel does not only provide MVC structure but also **Service Container** which resolves dependencies beautifully. The structure of Lumen and Laravel is much more than one design pattern but it utilizes different design patterns nicely. So, let's see what else Lumen provides and look into Service container and many other topics.

Separate configurations

In Chapter 4, *Reviewing Design Flaws and Security Threats*, we saw that configurations should be separate than implementation so Lumen does that for us. It has separate configuration files. In fact, it has a separate .env file that can be different in different environments. Other than the .env file, there is a configurations file where configuration related to different packages are stored, things like package registration or alias and so on.

 Please note that you probably don't see the .env file on Mac or Linux at first because it starts from the dot, so it will be hidden. You will need to make hidden files shown, and then you will see the .env file there.

Router

Lumen has better routing capabilities. It not only lets you tell which URLs should be served by which controller but also lets you tell which URLs with which HTTP Method should be served by which controller and which method of the controller. In fact, most of the HTTP methods that we use in the RESTful convention can be specified in Lumen.

While creating RESTful web service for our blog example, we will see code examples as well.

Middle-wares

Middle-ware is something that can come before or after serving a request by the controller. Many tasks can be performed in middle-wares, like authentication middle-ware, validation middle-ware and so on.

There are some middle-wares which come with Lumen itself, while we can also write our own middle-ware to serve our purpose.

Service Container and Dependency Injection

A service container is a tool provided for dependency injection and dependency resolution. Developers just tell which class should be injected where, and the service container resolves and injects that dependency.

Dependency injection can be used for resolving any dependency of a class if its object is created through the application service container, not through the new keyword in the application.

For example, the Lumen service container is used to resolve all Lumen controllers. So, if they need any dependency, the service container is responsible for resolving that. For better understanding consider the following example:

```
class PostController extends Post
{
    public function __construct(Post $post){
        //do something with $post
    }
}
```

In the preceding example, I have just mentioned the simple Controller class, where the Post class is being injected in the PostController constructor. If we already have another object which we want to be injected instead of the actual Post object, we can also do so.

You can simply do it using the following code from anywhere before dependencies are resolved:

```
$ourCustomerPost = new OurCustomPost();
$this->app->instance("\Post", $ourCustomerPost);
```

So now, if Post will be type hinted in a class' constructor or method then the object of OurCustomPost class will be injected there. This is because $this->app->instance("\Post", $ourCustomerPost) is telling the service container that if someone asks for an instance of \Post then give them $ourCustomerPost.

Note, other than controller resolution, we can also create an object in the following way if we want the service container to inject dependencies:

```
$postController = $this->app->make('PostController');
```

So here, PostController will be resolved in the same way as controllers are resolved by Lumen itself. Please note that we are using the term *Lumen* because we are talking about Lumen but most of this stuff is the same in both Lumen and Laravel.

Don't worry if this sounds a bit overwhelming, you will start understanding this once you start using Lumen or Laravel and do practical work in it.

HTTP responses

Lumen has built-in support for sending different types of responses, HTTP status codes and response headers. This is something that we previously discussed as important. It is even more important for web services because web services are used by a machine, on a human. The machine should be able to know what the response type is and what the status code is. This is not only useful to tell whether there is error or success but also to tell what type of error has occurred. You can look into this in more detail at `https://lumen.laravel.com/docs/5.4/responses`.

Validation

Lumen also comes with support for Validation as well; not only validation support but also built-in validation rules that you can start using. However, if you need some custom validation logic for some field, you can always write that as well. We will look into that while creating our RESTful web service.

Eloquent ORM

Lumen comes with an ORM tool named Eloquent. For ease of understanding, you can consider it as a database related high-level libraries by which you can get data without going into a lot of detail based on relationships. We will shortly look into it in detail while we use it.

Database migration and seeding

Nowadays, a developer is not always supposed to create databases using SQL or database tool. There should be something in the code which can be under Version Control System and every developer in the team can run on his/her system or on the server. This something is nowadays called migration. Another benefit of writing migration is that it is not for one specific database. The same migration can work on both MySQL and PostgreSQL. Migrations are about structural changes in the database.

A migration is for database table creation or modifications, or different constraints or indexes creation. In the same way, Seeders are there to insert data in the database.

Unit testing

Unit testing is also a very important for ensuring the quality of code, and Lumen provides support for that as well. We will not be writing the test in this chapter, but we will write it in a later chapter.

Note that we haven't seen each and every thing that comes with Lumen, we have just seen some components which we may need to know in order to make RESTful web services in Lumen. For further details of Lumen, you can simply consult its documentation: `https://lumen.laravel.com/docs/5.4`.

Installing Lumen

To install Lumen, if you have composer installed then simply run this:

```
composer create-project --prefer-dist laravel/lumen blog
```

This will create a directory named `blog` which has the Lumen installation in it. In case you find any difficulty, see the Lumen installation docs here: `https://lumen.laravel.com/docs/5.4`.

I suggest that after installation, you go and look at the directory structure of this Lumen project named blog, as it will make more sense when we will be performing different tasks.

Configuration

If you look in the installation directory where we installed Lumen, in our case it was `blog`, you will see a `.env` file. Lumen keeps configurations in the `.env` file. You can see there is an option `APP_KEY=` if this is not yet set in the `.env` file, set it. This just needs to be set to a random string that has a 32 character length.

 As `.env` file starts with a dot, in Linux or Mac, this file may be hidden. In order to see this file, you need to see hidden files as well.

And then, to run Lumen simply use the following command:

```
php -S localhost:8000 -t public
```

As you can see, we are using a PHP built-in server and giving the path of the `public` directory in our project. This is because the entry point is `public/index.php`. Then, on `http://localhost:8000/`, you should see `Lumen (5.4.6) (Laravel Components 5.4.*)`.

If you ever see the error `Class 'Memcached' not found`, this means you don't have Memcached installed and Lumen is trying to use it somewhere. If you don't need Memcached, you can simply go to `.env` file and change `CACHE_DRIVER=file`.

Now that we have Lumen installed and configured, we will create the same RESTful web services for the blog example in Lumen.

One more thing you should do is uncomment following in `bootstrap/app.php`.

```
//$app->withFacades();

//$app->withEloquent();
```

As was previously commented, with these features not available, Lumen can be faster. But we uncommented it because we also need to utilize some capabilities of Lumen. So what, exactly, do these two lines do? The first one enables use of Facades. We enabled it because we will need some packages which need Facade. The second one enables usage of the Eloquent ORM that comes with Laravel and Lumen. Eloquent isn't enabled by default for the sake of performance. However, Eloquent is a very important component that we shouldn't avoid, not even for the sake of performance, unless performance is critical for us and it is slowing down because of Eloquent. In my opinion, we shouldn't compromise clarity for performance unless it is critical.

Setting up the database

We need to set up our database for the blog. In fact, we already did set this up in Chapter 3, *Creating Restful Endpoints*. We can use that database here as well. In fact, we will have the same DB structure, so we can easily use the same DB, but this is not recommended. In Lumen, we use migrations to create DB structure. It is not mandatory but it is useful so you can write migration once and use it to create DB structure anywhere. This purpose can be served by SQL files but the beauty of migration is that it works across different RDBMS as well. So create a DB manually, and name it `blog`. Now, we will write migration for structure.

Writing migrations

To create migration files in Lumen, we can use this command in the `blog` directory to create migration file:

```
php artisan make:migration create_users_table
```

You will see something similar to this:

```
Created Migration: 2017_06_23_180043_create_users_table
```

and a file with this name will be created in the `/blog/database/migrations` directory. In this file, we can write migration code for the Users table. If you open the file and look into it, there are 2 methods in it: `up()` and `down()`. `up()` method executes when it has to run migration while `down()` executes when it has to rollback migration.

Here is the content of this User table creation migration file:

```php
<?php

use Illuminate\Database\Migrations\Migration;
use Illuminate\Database\Schema\Blueprint;

class CreateUsersTable extends Migration {

    /**
     * Run the migrations.
     *
     * @return void
     */
    public function up()
    {
        Schema::create('users', function(Blueprint $table)
        {
            $table->integer('id', true);
            $table->string('name', 100);
            $table->string('email', 50)->unique('email_unique');
            $table->string('password', 100);
            $table->timestamps();
        });
    }


    /**
     * Reverse the migrations.
     *
     * @return void
```

```
*/
public function down()
{
    Schema::drop('users');
}

}
```

Here in the `up()` method, we have called the create method while passing a function in it. And that function has code to add fields. If you want to know more about fields and table creation through migration, you can have a look at `https://laravel.com/docs/5.4/migrations#tables`.

However, before running the command to generate migration from the database, you should go to your `.env` file and add your DB name and credentials. In order to run the migration, run this command:

`php artisan migrate`

This will run the migration, and will create two tables: a migrations table and a Users table. The Users table was created as the result of the previously mentioned code, while the migrations table was created by Laravel/Lumen as it is where it keeps the record of migrations which are run. This table is created the first time, and will always have more data in it whenever migrations run.

 Please note that before running migration you should have MySQL or some other database installed and configured in the `.env` file. Otherwise, if there is no database installed or set up, then migration will not work.

Now, you can create posts and comments table creation migration files in the same way. Following is the content of the posts and comments table creation migration files respectively.

Posts migration file content:

```php
<?php

use Illuminate\Database\Migrations\Migration;
use Illuminate\Database\Schema\Blueprint;

class CreatePostsTable extends Migration {

    /**
     * Run the migrations.
     *
```

```php
     * @return void
     */
    public function up()
    {
        Schema::create('posts', function(Blueprint $table)
        {
            $table->integer('id', true);
            $table->string('title', 100);
            $table->enum('status',
array('draft','published'))->default('draft');
            $table->text('content', 65535);
            $table->integer('user_id')->index('user_id_foreign');

            $table->timestamps();
        });
    }


    /**
     * Reverse the migrations.
     *
     * @return void
     */
    public function down()
    {
        Schema::drop('posts');
    }

}
```

And here is the comments table creation migration file:

```php
<?php

use Illuminate\Database\Migrations\Migration;
use Illuminate\Database\Schema\Blueprint;

class CreateCommentsTable extends Migration {

    /**
     * Run the migrations.
     *
     * @return void
     */
    public function up()
    {
        Schema::create('comments', function(Blueprint $table)
        {
```

```
        $table->integer('id', true);
        $table->string('comment', 250);
        $table->integer('post_id')->index('post_id');
        $table->integer('user_id')->index('user_id');

        $table->timestamps();
    });
}


/**
 * Reverse the migrations.
 *
 * @return void
 */
public function down()
{
    Schema::drop('comments');
}

}
```

After having the preceding two files, run the following command again:

```
php artisan migrate
```

The preceding command will only execute new migration files which were not yet executed. With that, you will have all three of these tables in the database. And as we will have these migrations as well, it will be easy to just run migrations again and have this schema in DB. You are probably thinking, "what is good about writing migrations?". The good part is that migrations make it easier to deploy it on any RDBMS because the code is Laravel migration code and not SQL code. Also, it is always easier to have such stuff in code so that multiple developers can get each other's migrations and run them on the fly.

If you remember, we also did some indexing and foreign key constraints. So, here is how we can do that in the migration way.

Create a new migration file using the command as we did before:

```
php artisan make:migration add_foreign_keys_to_comments_table
```

This will create a migration file for comments table indexes. Let's add content to this file:

```php
<?php

use Illuminate\Database\Migrations\Migration;
use Illuminate\Database\Schema\Blueprint;

class AddForeignKeysToCommentsTable extends Migration {

    /**
     * Run the migrations.
     *
     * @return void
     */
    public function up()
    {
        Schema::table('comments', function(Blueprint $table)
        {
            $table->foreign('post_id',
'post_id_comment_foreign')->references('id')->on('posts')->onUpdate('RESTRI
CT')->onDelete('RESTRICT');
            $table->foreign('post_id',
'post_id_foreign')->references('id')->on('posts')->onUpdate('RESTRICT')->on
Delete('RESTRICT');
            $table->foreign('user_id',
'user_id_comment_foreign')->references('id')->on('users')->onUpdate('RESTRI
CT')->onDelete('RESTRICT');
        });
    }


    /**
     * Reverse the migrations.
     *
     * @return void
     */
    public function down()
    {
        Schema::table('comments', function(Blueprint $table)
        {
            $table->dropForeign('post_id_comment_foreign');
            $table->dropForeign('post_id_foreign');
            $table->dropForeign('user_id_comment_foreign');
        });
    }

}
```

In the same way, create a migration file for posts indexes. Here is the content of the file:

```php
<?php

use Illuminate\Database\Migrations\Migration;
use Illuminate\Database\Schema\Blueprint;

class AddForeignKeysToPostsTable extends Migration {

    /**
     * Run the migrations.
     *
     * @return void
     */
    public function up()
    {
        Schema::table('posts', function(Blueprint $table)
        {
            $table->foreign('user_id',
'user_id_foreign')->references('id')->on('users')->onUpdate('RESTRICT')->on
Delete('RESTRICT');
        });
    }


    /**
     * Reverse the migrations.
     *
     * @return void
     */
    public function down()
    {
        Schema::table('posts', function(Blueprint $table)
        {
            $table->dropForeign('user_id_foreign');
        });
    }

}
```

In the preceding indexes files code, there is some code that is a bit complex and needs our attention:

```php
$table->foreign('user_id',
'user_id_foreign')->references('id')->on('users')->onUpdate('RESTRICT')->on
Delete('RESTRICT');
```

Here, the `foreign()` method accepts the field name and name of the index. Then, the `references()` method accepts the foreign key field name in the parent table, and the `on()` method parameter is the referenced table name (in our case, it is the users table). And then, the rest of the two methods `onUpdate()` and `onDelete()` tell the user what to do on update and delete respectively. If you are not comfortable with migration syntax, it is fine; you just need to look at the Lumen/Laravel migration documentation. In fact, I recommend that you pause for a moment and look at the migration related documentation: `https://laravel.com/docs/5.4/migrations`.

Now, to have these migrations effective in the database, we need to run migrations again so that new migrations can execute and we can have changes reflected in the database. So run:

```
php artisan migrate
```

With that, we are done with migration. We can now insert some data in these tables through seeds, but we don't need it yet, so skipping writing seeds for now.

Writing RESTful web service endpoints

Now, it is time to actually start writing the endpoints that we discussed in Chapter 1, *RESTful Web Services, Introduction and Motivation*, and wrote in plain Vanilla PHP in Chapter 3, *Creating Restful Endpoints*. So let's do that.

As it has a Controller and Model layer, we will start writing API from the Controller layer which will serve different endpoints. For the first controller, what we are going to write is `PostController`.

Writing the first controller

Technically, this is not the first controller, as Lumen comes with 2 controllers which you can find in the `/<our blog project path>/app/Http/Controllers/` directory. But this is our first controller that we are going to write. In Laravel (the big brother of Lumen), we don't need to go and create a controller because there are commands for that, but for Lumen those commands are not available. As these commands are not mandatory but very handy, it is better if we make those commands available.

To use the extra features that we don't get with Lumen (some of which come in Laravel already), we need to install a package. Right now, the package we need to install is `flipbox/lumen-generator`. More information about this package can be found at `https://packagist.org/packages/flipbox/lumen-generator`.

As we have seen in the previous chapter, we install packages through composer, so let's install it:

```
composer require --dev flipbox/lumen-generator
```

You can see that I have added a `--dev` flag there. I did this to avoid using it on production, because this way it will be added in the `require --dev` section in `composer.json`.

Anyway, once this is installed, you can register its `ServiceProvider` in `bootstrap/app.php`:

```
if ($app->environment() !== 'production') {
$app->register(Flipbox\LumenGenerator\LumenGeneratorServiceProvider::class)
;
}
```

Now, you can see that we have lot more commands available. You can see it by running:

```
php artisan migrate
```

So, let's create a controller with a command. Note, we didn't install it only for creating controller but it will be very handy when you will be working with it. Anyway, let's create a controller with the following command:

```
php artisan make:controller PostController --resource
```

It will create a controller at `app/Http/Controllers/PostController.php`. This command will not only create `PostController` but will also add REST Resource related methods as well. Open a file and look into it.

Here is the content that it generated:

```php
<?php

namespace App\Http\Controllers;

use Illuminate\Http\Request;

class PostController extends Controller
{
    /**
     * Display a listing of the resource.
     *
     * @return \Illuminate\Http\Response
     */
    public function index()
    {
```

```
        //
    }

    /**
     * Store a newly created resource in storage.
     *
     * @param  \Illuminate\Http\Request  $request
     * @return \Illuminate\Http\Response
     */
    public function store(Request $request)
    {
        //
    }

    /**
     * Display the specified resource.
     *
     * @param  int  $id
     * @return \Illuminate\Http\Response
     */
    public function show($id)
    {
        //
    }

    /**
     * Update the specified resource in storage.
     *
     * @param  \Illuminate\Http\Request  $request
     * @param  int  $id
     * @return \Illuminate\Http\Response
     */
    public function update(Request $request, $id)
    {
        //
    }

    /**
     * Remove the specified resource from storage.
     *
     * @param  int  $id
     * @return \Illuminate\Http\Response
     */
    public function destroy($id)
    {
        //
    }
}
```

These methods were generated because we added the flag `--resource`. If you are wondering from where did I get the knowledge of this flag, because it isn't listed on package page, I got it from Laravel's Controller documentation at `https://laravel.com/docs/5.4/controllers#resource-controllers`. However, as these commands are working because of a third party package, there can be a difference in Laravel documentation and these command's actual behavior, but as these were done to replicate those Laravel commands for Lumen, most probably they will be very similar.

Anyway, we have `PostController` with methods in it. Let's implement these methods one by one.

However, note that in Lumen and Laravel, unlike other PHP MVC frameworks, every URL should be told in routes or else it will not be accessible. Routes are a sort of only entry point, unlike other frameworks like `CodeIgniter` where the route is optional. In Lumen, routes are mandatory. In other words, every method of Controller will only be accessible through routes.

So before proceeding with `PostController`, let's add routes for post endpoints, otherwise `PostController` will be of no use.

Lumen routes

In Lumen, by default, routes live in `/routes/web.php`. I said by default because this path can be changed. Anyway, go to `routes/web.php` and look into it. You will see that it is returning a response by itself and not pointing towards any controller. So, you should know that it is up to route whether it returns a response or uses the controller for that. However, note that returning a response from route closure only makes sense if there isn't much logic involved. In our case, we will be mostly using controllers.

Here is how our routes will look when we add our first route:

```php
<?php

/*
|--------------------------------------------------------------
| Application Routes
|--------------------------------------------------------------
|
| Here is where you can register all of the routes for an application.
| It is a breeze. Simply tell Lumen the URIs it should respond to
| and give it the Closure to call when that URI is requested.
|
*/
```

```php
$app->get('/', function () use ($app) {
    return $app->version();
});

$app->get('/api/posts', [
    'uses' => 'PostController@index',
    'as' => 'list_posts'
]);
```

The code in bold is written by us. Here, get in `$app->get()` is used to specify the HTTP Method. It could be `$app->post()` but we used `$app->get()` to specify that the GET method is accepted. Then, there are 2 parameters in this method that you can see in the preceding code. First is the route pattern while the second parameter is an associative array which has the controller and the method in the `uses` key and route name in the `as` key: means after the domain or project URLs if `api/posts/` is an URL, it should be served by the `index()` method of `PostController`. While the route name is just there, if you want to specify route URLs by name in code then it is useful.

Now to check if our route is correct and getting a response from Controller's index method, let's add something to the index method of `PostController`. Here is what we have added, for now, just to test our route:

```php
public function index()
{
    return ['response' =>
        [
            'id' => 1,
            'title' => 'Some Post',
            'body' => 'Here is post body'
        ]
    ];
}
```

Now, try running this code. Before anything else, you need to use a PHP built-in server. Go to the `blog` directory where the whole code is and run:

```
php -S localhost:8000 -t public
```

Then, from the browser, hit: `http://localhost:8000/api/posts` and you will see the following response:

```
{"response":{"id":1,"title":"Some Post","body":"Here is post body"}}
```

As you can see, our route worked and served from the `index()` method of `PostController`, and if you return an array then Lumen converts it into JSON and returns it as JSON.

To further see the list of routes that certain URLs map to a particular controller's particular method, simply run:

```
php artisan route:list
```

You will see the detail of routes telling you which URLs pattern is associated with which piece of code.

REST resource

This was a very basic example of the route and served from a `PostController` method. However, if you look at `PostController`, it has 4 more methods, and we need to serve 4 more endpoints as we discussed in Chapter 1, *RESTful Web Services, Introduction and Motivation*, and implemented in Chapter 3, *Creating Restful Endpoints*. So, we need to do the same thing in Lumen for other 4 methods. To map 4 endpoints with these 4 methods, we shouldn't need 4 more routes. We can simply add a resource-based route which will map REST based URL patterns to all methods in `PostController`.

As we created `PostController` through the command line, it created a Resource Controller which means it has the necessary methods to serve RESTful endpoints. So in `routes/web.php` file, we should simply replace code we previously wrote with the resource route. Now, we should be able to map all RESTful endpoints to `PostController` methods by having this statement in the routes file:

```
$app->resource('api/posts', 'PostController');
```

Unfortunately, this resource route is available in Laravel but not in Lumen. Lumen uses a different router for better performance. However, this resource method is also very handy, and if we have 4-5 more RESTful resources, we can map all their endpoints in just 4-5 statements instead of 16-20 statements. So, here is a small trick to have this resource route sort of thing available in Lumen. You can add this custom method to the same route file.

```
function resource($uri, $controller)
{
    //$verbs = ['GET', 'HEAD', 'POST', 'PUT', 'PATCH', 'DELETE'];

    global $app;

    $app->get($uri, $controller.'@index');
```

```
        $app->post($uri, $controller.'@store');

        $app->get($uri.'/{id}', $controller.'@show');
        $app->put($uri.'/{id}', $controller.'@update');
        $app->patch($uri.'/{id}', $controller.'@update');

        $app->delete($uri.'/{id}', $controller.'@destroy');
    }
```

So overall, our route file will look like this:

```
<?php

/*
|--------------------------------------------------------------------
| Application Routes
|--------------------------------------------------------------------
|
| Here is where you can register all of the routes for an application.
| It is a breeze. Simply tell Lumen the URIs it should respond to
| and give it the Closure to call when that URI is requested.
|
*/


function resource($uri, $controller)
{
    //$verbs = ['GET', 'HEAD', 'POST', 'PUT', 'PATCH', 'DELETE'];
    global $app;
    $app->get($uri, $controller.'@index');
    $app->post($uri, $controller.'@store');
    $app->get($uri.'/{id}', $controller.'@show');
    $app->put($uri.'/{id}', $controller.'@update');
    $app->patch($uri.'/{id}', $controller.'@update');
    $app->delete($uri.'/{id}', $controller.'@destroy');
}


$app->get('/', function () use ($app) {
    return $app->version();
});


resource('api/posts', 'PostController');
```

The code written in bold is added by us. So, as you can see we have defined the
resource() function in the routes file once, and we can use it for all REST resource routes.
And then on the last line, we used the resource function to map all of the api/posts
endpoints to PostController respective methods.

Now you can test it, by hitting `http://localhost:8000/api/posts`. We can't test other endpoints right now because we haven't written any code in `PostController` other methods. However, you can see what routes exist by using this command:

```
php artisan route:list
```

In our case, this command will result in something like this on the command line:

```
rshaariz@naariz-HP-ProBook-440-G1:~/Dropbox/book/code/chapter6/blog$ php artisanoute:list
+--------+----------------+------------+-------------------------------------------+---------+------------+
| Verb   | Path           | NamedRoute | Controller                                | Action  | Middleware |
+--------+----------------+------------+-------------------------------------------+---------+------------+
| GET    | /              |            | None                                      | Closure |            |
| GET    | /api/posts     |            | App\Http\Controllers\PostController       | index   |            |
| POST   | /api/posts     |            | App\Http\Controllers\PostController       | store   |            |
| GET    | /api/posts/{id}|            | App\Http\Controllers\PostController       | show    |            |
| PUT    | /api/posts/{id}|            | App\Http\Controllers\PostController       | update  |            |
| PATCH  | /api/posts/{id}|            | App\Http\Controllers\PostController       | update  |            |
| DELETE | /api/posts/{id}|            | App\Http\Controllers\PostController       | destroy |            |
+--------+----------------+------------+-------------------------------------------+---------+------------+
```

Here, we can see this is mapping paths to `PostController` methods exactly based on the RESTful Resource convention that we discussed in `Chapter 1`, *RESTful Web Services, Introduction and Motivation*. So now, for posts endpoints we are done with routing. Now we need to add code in Controller so it can add data to the database as well as fetch from the database. The next step is to create a Model layer and use that in Controller and return a proper response.

Eloquent ORM (model layer)

Eloquent is an ORM that comes with Laravel and Lumen. It is responsible for database related operations as well as database relationships. **ORM (Object Relational Mapping)** basically maps objects with relations (tables) in the database. Not only that, based on the relationship you can get data of one table on the base of another table's relationship without going at the low-level detail. This not only saves our time but also keeps our code cleaner.

Creating models

We are now going to create models. Model layer is related to the database, so we will also mention database relationships in them. Let's create models for all three tables that we have. The model names will be `User`, `Post` and `Comment`, relating to the `users`, `posts` and `comments` tables.

We don't need to create a User model and it comes with Lumen. To create Post and Comment models, let's run the following command that became available to us by using that `flipbox/lumen-generator` package. Run the following commands to make models:

This will create a `Post` model in the `app` directory:

```
php artisan make:model Post
```

This will create the `Comment` model in the `app` directory:

```
php artisan make:model Comment
```

If you look into these model files, you will find that these are classes inherited by the Eloquent Model; so, these models are Eloquent based models and have characteristics of Eloquent Model.

Note, as per Eloquent convention, if the model's name is Post, the table's name will be posts, the plural of the model's name. Similarly, for the Comment Model, it will be the comments table. We can override this if our tables names are different, but we are not doing so because in our case, our table and Model names are according to the same convention.

Eloquent is a big topic to discuss, however we are just going to use it to make our API, so I will limit discussion to Eloquent's usage in serving our purpose. And I think this makes sense because a lot of detail is already in Eloquent's documentation, so for further details about Eloquent, please consult Eloquent's documentation here: `https://laravel.com/docs/5.4/eloquent`.

Eloquent relationships

In the Model layer, especially when inheriting from ORM, there are 2 important things:

- We should have Models so we can access data through them
- We should specify relationships so we can utilize ORM's full capabilities

For just accessing data without writing a query, we can use Query Builder as well. But, relationships advantage is that it comes only with ORM usage. So, let's specify all of the models' relationships.

First of all, let's specify User's relationships. As the user can have many posts and the user can have many comments, the User model will have the `hasMany` relationship with both Post and Comment models. This is what the User model will look like after specifying the relationship:

```php
<?php

namespace App;

use Illuminate\Auth\Authenticatable;
use Laravel\Lumen\Auth\Authorizable;
use Illuminate\Database\Eloquent\Model;
use Illuminate\Contracts\Auth\Authenticatable as AuthenticatableContract;
use Illuminate\Contracts\Auth\Access\Authorizable as AuthorizableContract;

class User extends Model implements AuthenticatableContract,
AuthorizableContract
{
    use Authenticatable, Authorizable;

    /**
     * The attributes that are mass assignable.
     *
     * @var array
     */
    protected $fillable = [
        'name', 'email',
    ];

    /**
     * The attributes excluded from the model's JSON form.
     *
     * @var array
     */
    protected $hidden = [
        'password',
    ];

    public function posts(){
        return $this->hasMany('App\Post');
    }

    public function comments(){
        return $this->hasMany('App\Comment');
    }
}
```

The only thing which we added to the User Model is these 2 methods in bold which are posts() and comments() specifying the relationship. Based on these methods, we can access a user's posts and comments data. Both of these methods tell us that User has many relationships with both the Post and Comment models.

Now, let's add a relationship in the Post model. As a post can have many comments, the Post model has many relationships with the Comment model. Meanwhile, the Post model has an inverse of many relationships with the User model and that inverse relationship is a belongsTo relationship. Here is the Post model code after adding relationship information.

```php
<?php

namespace App;

use Illuminate\Database\Eloquent\Model;

class Post extends Model
{
    public function comments(){
        return $this->hasMany('App\Comment');
    }

    public function user(){
        return $this->belongsTo('App\User');
    }
}
```

As you can see, we have specified Post's relationship with the User and Comment models. Now, here is the Comment model with relationships.

```php
<?php

namespace App;

use Illuminate\Database\Eloquent\Model;

class Comment extends Model
{
    public function post(){
        return $this->belongsTo("App\Post");
    }

    public function user(){
        return $this->belongsTo("App\User");
```

```
    }
}
```

As you can see, for both the `Post` and `User` models, comments have a `belongsTo` relationship that is an inverse of `hasMany()`.

So, now we have specified relationships. It is time to implement `PostController` methods.

Controller Implementation

Let's first add proper code in the `PostController index()` method that will return actual data. But to see data coming in response, it is better to insert some dummy data in the users, posts and comments tables. A better way to do this is to write seeds for that. However, if you don't want to look into how to write seeds then you can insert it manually for now.

Here is an implementation of the `index()` method:

```
public function index(\App\Post $post)
{
    return $post->paginate(20);
}
```

Here, `paginate(20)` means that it will return a paginated result with the limit of 20. And as you can see, we have used dependency injection to get the `Post` object. This is something that we have already discussed in this chapter.

Similarly, we will have `PostController` other methods implemented here. This is what the `PostController` code will look like:

```
<?php

namespace App\Http\Controllers;

use Illuminate\Http\Request;

class PostController extends Controller
{

    public function __construct(\App\Post $post)
    {
        $this->post = $post;
    }
```

```php
/**
 * Display a listing of the resource.
 *
 * @return \Illuminate\Http\Response
 */
public function index()
{
    return $this->post->paginate(20);
}

/**
 * Store a newly created resource in storage.
 *
 * @param  \Illuminate\Http\Request  $request
 * @return \Illuminate\Http\Response
 */
public function store(Request $request)
{
    $input = $request->all();
    $this->post->create($input);

    return [
        'data' => $input
    ];
}

/**
 * Display the specified resource.
 *
 * @param  int  $id
 * @return \Illuminate\Http\Response
 */
public function show($id)
{
    return $this->post->find($id);
}

/**
 * Update the specified resource in storage.
 *
 * @param  \Illuminate\Http\Request  $request
 * @param  int  $id
 * @return \Illuminate\Http\Response
 */
public function update(Request $request, $id)
{
    $input = $request->all();
    $this->post->where('id', $id)->update($input);
```

```
        return $this->post->find($id);
    }

    /**
     * Remove the specified resource from storage.
     *
     * @param  int   $id
     * @return \Illuminate\Http\Response
     */
    public function destroy($id)
    {
        $post = $this->post->destroy($id);

        return ['message' => 'deleted successfully', 'post_id' => $post];
    }
}
```

As you can see, we are using the Post model and using its methods to perform different operations. Lumen's variable and function names make it easier to understand what is going on, but if you are wondering what Eloquent methods you can use, to see these methods check Eloquent at: `https://laravel.com/docs/5.4/eloquent`.

If you don't find any of Eloquent method's documentation there note that, a lot of functions that we used are of Query Builder. So see query builder documentation as well, visit `https://laravel.com/docs/5.4/queries`.

As `CommentController` implementation will be similar, I would suggest you to implement `CommentController` by yourself, because you will actually learn when you do it by yourself.

What we are missing?

Are we done with making Controllers that serves RESTful resources endpoints? Actually no, we have missed many things. We just created basic RESTful web service, which can work just to give you an idea of how we can make it using Lumen, but we have missed many things. So, let's look at them and do them one by one.

Validation and negative cases?

First, we are only dealing with positive cases: that means we are not considering what happens if the request is not according to our assumption. What if the user is sending data with the wrong method? What if a record doesn't exist with the ID that the user is passing on?

In short, we are not yet handling all that, but there are things that Lumen is handling for us already.

If you try to hit endpoint URLs, `http://localhost:8000/api/posts/1` with the POST method, then, it is an invalid method. On those URLs, we can only send a request with GET, PUT or PATCH. With GET, it will trigger the PostController show() method while PUT or PATCH will trigger the update() method. But the POST method shouldn't be allowed. And in fact, if you try to send a request on these URLs with the POST method, it will not work, and you will also get a Method Not Allowed error just like it should be. So by defining our routes once, Lumen will deal with such errors by itself.

In the same way, Lumen will invalidate wrong URLs or wrong HTTP methods and URL combinations.

Other than that, we are not going to make it handle each and every case, but let's look at important stuff that we must deal with; stuff without which our work couldn't be completed.

So, let's see what we have missed in each method of PostController regarding validation or missing use cases.

/api/posts with GET method

Here is the response of /api/posts endpoint (in my case, there is only one record in DB):

```
{
    "current_page":1,
    "data":[
        {
            "id":1,
            "title":"test",
            "status":"draft",
            "content":"test post",
            "user_id":2
        }
    ],
    "from":1,
```

```
    "last_page":1,
    "next_page_url":null,
    "path":"http:\/\/localhost:8000\/api\/posts",
    "per_page":20,
    "prev_page_url":null,
    "to":1,
    "total":1
}
```

If you recall the response that we saw in Chapter 1, *RESTful Web Services, Introduction and Motivation*, you will see that we are getting most of the information that we discussed but we are getting it in a different format. Although that is perfectly fine as it is giving enough information, here is how we can make it similar to what we decided.

Here is what the index() method will become:

```
public function index()
{
    $posts = $this->post->paginate(20);
    $data = $posts['data'];

    $response = [
        'data' => $data,
        'total_count' => $posts['total'],
        'limit' => $posts['per_page'],
        'pagination' => [
            'next_page' => $posts['next_page_url'],
            'current_page' => $posts['current_page']
        ]
    ];

    return $response;
}
```

The most important thing was that all the information at the root level of response isn't clean. We should eliminate the stuff that harms clarity because programmers' productivity can be affected if a programmer needs to spend more time just to understand something. We should have pagination related information under a separate attribute, which can be pagination or meta, so that the programmer can easily see data and other attributes.

We did it, but we did it manually. For now, let's be done with it. In the next chapter, we will see what is wrong with this, why we called it manually, and what we can do about it.

/api/posts with the POST method

This will trigger the `PostController::store()` method. The thing we have missed is validation. In fact, Lumen provides us validation support as well as some built-in validation rules. Lumen validation is very similar to Laravel, with some differences. I would suggest that you have a look at Laravel's validation documentation, at `https://laravel.com/docs/5.4/validation`, and Lumen's validation differences with Laravel: `https://lumen.laravel.com/docs/5.4/validation`.

Here, we have added validation in `store()`, so look at the code after adding validation and we will then discuss it:

```
public function store(Request $request)
{
    $input = $request->all();

    $validationRules = [
        'content' => 'required|min:1',
        'title' => 'required|min:1',
        'status' => 'required|in:draft,published',
        'user_id' => 'required|exists:users,id'
    ];

    $validator = \Validator::make($input, $validationRules);
    if ($validator->fails()) {
        return new \Illuminate\Http\JsonResponse(
            [
                'errors' => $validator->errors()
            ], \Illuminate\Http\Response::HTTP_BAD_REQUEST
        );
    }

$post = $this->post->create($input);

return [
'data' => $post
];
}
```

Here we are doing 3 things:

1. First, we have set the following validation rules:
   1. For `content` and `title`, these fields will be required and will be a minimum of 1 character long.
   2. For `status`, it is required and its value can be either published or draft as it is set as ENUM in the database.
   3. `user_id` is required and it should exist in the `users` table's `id` field.
2. Then, we made a validator object based on validation rules and input, and check if validator fails. Otherwise, we will keep proceeding.
3. If the validator fails, it returns an error manually. It is returning the same error description that it gets from the validator while returning an appropriate response code manually. And that's why we have used `\Illuminate\Http\JsonResponse`. The first parameter is the response body while the second parameter is the response code. And instead of writing 400 error code, we can use a constant in `\Illuminate\Http\Response`. So we will not need to remember the response codes, and someone reading our code will not need to know what the 400 status code is.

 Please note that Error code, response code, and HTTP code represent the same thing. So don't get confused if you see them, they are used interchangeably in this book.

/api/posts/1 with the GET method

This will be served from the `show($id)` method. In our show method, we are just getting the record and returning, but what if ID coming in the `show()` method that is passed in URLs is incorrect, or records indicate that ID doesn't exist? So, we just need to place a check to make sure that it returns a 404 error, if a post is not found with that ID. Our code for the `show()` method will look like this:

```
public function show($id)
{
    $post = $this->post->find($id);

    if(!$post) {
        abort(404);
    }
```

```
            return $post;
    }
```

The `abort()` method will stop execution with an error code passed to it. In this case, it will simply give a 404 Not Found Error.

/api/posts/1 with the PATCH/PUT method

It will be served by the `update()` method. Again, it is based on ID provided, so we need to check if that ID is valid or not. So here is what we will do:

```
public function update(Request $request, $id)
{
    $input = $request->all();

    $post = $this->post->find($id);

    if(!$post) {
        abort(404);
    }

    $post->fill($input);
    $post->save();

    return $post;
}
```

Here, we have used model's `fill()` method, which will assign Post model with fields and values in $input and will then save it with the `save()` method. In Laravel documentation, you can see Insert and Update using Eloquent in different ways, which can be handy in different places: `https://laravel.com/docs/5.4/eloquent#inserting-and-updating-models`.

Sometimes, you will see a Laravel documentation link instead of Lumen. It is because Lumen is mostly using the same code as Laravel. The documentation for all those components are mostly written in Laravel's documentation and it isn't replicated in Lumen documentation, so Lumen documentation is good where Lumen is different from Laravel.

So that is what we have to do in the `update()` method.

/api/posts/1 with the DELETE method

The delete operation will be served by destroy ($id). Again, it depends on ID coming from an API user, so we need to place a similar check as we placed for update () and show (). Here is what it will look like:

```php
public function destroy($id)
{
    $post = $this->post->find($id);

    if(!$post) {
        abort(404);
    }

    $post->delete();

    return ['message' => 'deleted successfully', 'post_id' => $id];
}
```

With that, our PostController will look like this:

```php
<?php

namespace App\Http\Controllers;

use Illuminate\Http\Request;
use Illuminate\Http\Response;
use Illuminate\Http\JsonResponse;

class PostController extends Controller
{

    public function __construct(\App\Post $post)
    {
        $this->post = $post;
    }

    /**
     * Display a listing of the resource.
     *
     * @return \Illuminate\Http\Response
     */
    public function index()
    {
        $posts = $this->post->paginate(20);
        $data = $posts['data'];

        $response = [
```

```
                'data' => $data,
                'total_count' => $posts['total'],
                'limit' => $posts['per_page'],
                'pagination' => [
                    'next_page' => $posts['next_page_url'],
                    'current_page' => $posts['current_page']
                ]
        ];

        return $response;
    }

    /**
     * Store a newly created resource in storage.
     *
     * @param  \Illuminate\Http\Request  $request
     * @return \Illuminate\Http\Response
     */
    public function store(Request $request)
    {
        $input = $request->all();

        $validationRules = [
            'content' => 'required|min:1',
            'title' => 'required|min:1',
            'status' => 'required|in:draft,published',
            'user_id' => 'required|exists:users,id'
        ];

        $validator = \Validator::make($input, $validationRules);
        if ($validator->fails()) {
            return new JsonResponse(
                [
                    'errors' => $validator->errors()
                ], Response::HTTP_BAD_REQUEST
            );
        }

        $post = $this->post->create($input);

        return [
            'data' => $post
        ];
    }

    /**
     * Display the specified resource.
     *
```

```
 * @param  int  $id
 * @return \Illuminate\Http\Response
 */
public function show($id)
{
    $post = $this->post->find($id);

    if(!$post) {
        abort(404);
    }

    return $post;
}

/**
 * Update the specified resource in storage.
 *
 * @param  \Illuminate\Http\Request  $request
 * @param  int  $id
 * @return \Illuminate\Http\Response
 */
public function update(Request $request, $id)
{
    $input = $request->all();

    $post = $this->post->find($id);

    if(!$post) {
        abort(404);
    }

    $post->fill($input);
    $post->save();

    return $post;
}

/**
 * Remove the specified resource from storage.
 *
 * @param  int  $id
 * @return \Illuminate\Http\Response
 */
public function destroy($id)
{
    $post = $this->post->find($id);

    if(!$post) {
```

```
            abort(404);
        }

        $post->delete();

        return ['message' => 'deleted successfully', 'post_id' => $id];
    }
}
```

We are now done with returning proper response codes and validation and so on.

User authentication

The other thing we are missing till now is user authentication. We are passing `user_id` in the input, and that is wrong. We did that because we didn't have user authentication. So, we need to have an authentication mechanism. However, in addition to authentication, we need to have a token-generation mechanism as well. In fact, we will also need to refresh token as well. Although we can do this by ourselves, we will install another external package.

Starting user authentication at the end of the chapter doesn't make much sense, so we will be dealing with user authentication in next chapter because there are different things associated with it.

Other missing elements

Other things that we are missing right now are listed as follows:

- API versioning
- Rate Limiting or Throttling
- Need of encryption
- Transformers or Serializes
  (This is to avoid making hard code manual return format inside the controller)

In the next chapter, we will deal with user authentication and the preceding mentioned elements, and will make some other improvements.

Comment Resource Implementation

I left comment endpoints implementation to you, because it is very much similar to Post endpoints implementation. However, as comment's two routes are different than others, just to give you an idea of what you need to implement, I am going to tell what you will add in the `routes` file so that you can implement `CommentController` accordingly. Here is the `routes/web.php` file:

```php
<?php

/*
|--------------------------------------------------------------
| Application Routes
|--------------------------------------------------------------
|
| Here is where you can register all of the routes for an application.
| It is a breeze. Simply tell Lumen the URIs it should respond to
| and give it the Closure to call when that URI is requested.
|
*/

function resource($uri, $controller, $except = [])
{
    //$verbs = ['GET', 'HEAD', 'POST', 'PUT', 'PATCH', 'DELETE'];

    global $app;

    if(!in_array('index', $except)){
        $app->get($uri, $controller.'@index');
    }

    if(!in_array('store', $except)) {
        $app->post($uri, $controller . '@store');
    }

    if(!in_array('show', $except)) {
        $app->get($uri . '/{id}', $controller . '@show');
    };

    if(!in_array('udpate', $except)) {
        $app->put($uri . '/{id}', $controller . '@update');
        $app->patch($uri . '/{id}', $controller . '@update');
    }

    if(!in_array('destroy', $except)) {
```

```
            $app->delete($uri . '/{id}', $controller . '@destroy');
    }
}


$app->get('/', function () use ($app) {
    return $app->version();
});


resource('api/posts', 'PostController');
resource('api/comments', 'CommentController', ['store','index']);

$app->post('api/posts/{id}/comments', $controller . '@store');
$app->get('api/posts/{id}/comments', $controller . '@index');
```

As you can see, we have added the $except array as an optional third argument in resource() so that if we don't want to generate some particular route for a resource, we can pass that in the $except array.

In CommentController, the code will be very similar to PostController, except that for store() and index(), post_id will be the first argument and will be used.

Summary

Till now, we have created RESTful web services endpoints in a micro-framework named Lumen. We created migrations, models and routes. I implemented PostController but left CommentController implementation for you. So, as we can see that lot of problems that we discussed related to implementation in Chapter 3, *Creating Restful Endpoints*, are solved already because of using a framework. And we are able to solve many other problems very easily. So, using the right framework and packages, we are able to work much faster.

We have also identified some missing elements, including user authentication. We will solve them in the next chapter. In the next chapter, we will improve our work from the code aspect as well.

In this chapter, we were mostly working with Lumen. We looked at it but we were trying to proceed to make our API and so we were not able to see each and every part of Lumen and its code in detail. So, it is a good idea to see Lumen's documentation: `https://lumen.laravel.com/docs/5.4/validation`.

For better understanding, you should look at Laravel's documentation, as some common components are explained mostly in Laravel's documentation: `https://laravel.com/docs/5.4`.

Other than the documentation of Laravel and Lumen, it is a very good idea and is recommended to go to `http://laracasts.com/` and see videos on Laravel. Don't worry if you don't find much stuff on Lumen, it is very similar to Laravel. Other than a few changes, they are pretty much same. To understand Laravel and/or Lumen, Lara casts is an excellent resource and is very popular in the Laravel community. Lara casts are mostly by Jeffrey Way. I learned a lot from him and hope that you will learn as well. It will not only teach you Laravel but also teach you how to develop something, and how you should do development.

7
Improving RESTful Web Services

In the previous chapter, we created RESTful web services in Lumen, and we identified some missing elements or improvements required. In this chapter, we will work on improving that and completing some missing elements. We will improve certain elements with respect to fulfilling loopholes and code quality.

We will cover the following topics in this chapter to improve our RESTful web service:

- Dingo, simplifying RESTful API development:
    - Installing and configuring Dingo API package
    - Simplifying routes
    - API versioning
    - Rate limiting
    - Internal requests
- Authentication and middleware
- Transformers
- Need of encryption:
    - SSL, different options
- Summary

Dingo, simplifying RESTful API development

Yes, you heard it right. I didn't say bingo. It's Dingo. Actually, Dingo API is a package for Laravel and Lumen that makes it a lot simpler to develop RESTful web services. It provides many features out of the box and many are what we saw in the previous chapter. Many of these features will make our existing code better and easier to understand and maintain. You can check out the Dingo API package at `https://github.com/dingo/api`.

Let's first install it, and we will keep looking at its benefits and features side by side while using them.

Installation and configuration

Simply install it through composer:

```
composer require dingo/api:1.0.x@dev
```

Probably, you are wondering what this `@dev` is. So, here is what the Dingo documentation says:

> *At this time, the package is still in a developmental stage and as such, does not have a stable release. You may need to set your minimum stability to dev.*

If you are still not sure about why we need to set minimum stability, then it is because of the default minimum stability for every package that is set to `stable`. So, if you rely on the `dev` package, then it should be explicitly specified, or it probably will not install it as minimum stability will not match with the package's actual stability status.

Once it is installed, you need to register it. Go to `bootstrap/app.php` and put this statement in this file somewhere before `return $app;`:

```
$app->register(Dingo\Api\Provider\LumenServiceProvider::class);
```

After doing this, there are a few variables you need to set in your `.env` file. Add them at the end of the `.env` file:

```
API_PREFIX=api
API_VERSION=v1
API_DEBUG=true
API_NAME="Blog API"
API_DEFAULT_FORMAT=json
```

Configuration is self-explanatory. Now, let's move forward.

Simplifying routes

If you look at the `routes/web.php` file where we put our routes, you can see that we wrote 54 lines of code for post and comment endpoints. With Dingo API, we can replace those 54 lines with just 10 lines of code, and it will be even more cleaner. So let's do that. Here is how your `routes/web.php` file should look:

```php
<?php

/*
|--------------------------------------------------------------
| Application Routes
|--------------------------------------------------------------
|
| Here is where you can register all of the routes for an application.
| It is a breeze. Simply tell Lumen the URIs it should respond to
| and give it the Closure to call when that URI is requested.
|
*/
$api = app('Dingo\Api\Routing\Router');

$api->version('v1', function ($api) {

    $api->resource('posts', "App\Http\Controllers\PostController");
    $api->resource('comments', "App\Http\Controllers\CommentController", [
        'except' => ['store', 'index']
    ]);

    $api->post('posts/{id}/comments',
'App\Http\Controllers\CommentController@store');

    $api->get('posts/{id}/comments',
'App\Http\Controllers\CommentController@index');
});

$app->get('/', function () use ($app) {
 return $app->version();
});
```

As you can see, we just got the object of the router in `$api`. However, this is Dingo API router, not Lumen's default router. As you can see, it has the `resource()` method available as we wanted, and we can mention unwanted methods in the `except` array. So overall, our routes are now very much simplified.

To see the exact routes for your application, run the following command:

```
php artisan route:list
```

API versioning

Probably, you have noticed that in the preceding code example in our route file, we already mentioned the API version as `v1`. It is because API versioning is important and Dingo provides us the facility to do so. It is useful to serve different endpoints from different versions. You can have another version group and can serve the same endpoint with different content. If there is the same endpoint under different versions, then it will pick the version that is mentioned in your `.env` file.

However, it is better to have version in URI. To do so, we can simply use the following prefix:

```
$api->version('v1', ['prefix' => 'api/v1'], function ($api) {

    $api->resource('posts', "App\Http\Controllers\PostController");
    $api->resource('comments', "App\Http\Controllers\CommentController", [
'except' => ['store', 'index']
]);

    $api->post('posts/{id}/comments',
'App\Http\Controllers\CommentController@store');

    $api->get('posts/{id}/comments',
'App\Http\Controllers\CommentController@index');
});
```

With that now, our routes will include version information in URI. This is a recommended approach. Because if someone is working with version 1 and we are going to change something in version 2, then the client using version 1 will not be affected if they are specifying the version number explicitly in their requests. So, our endpoint URLs will be something like this:

```
http://localhost:8000/api/v1/posts
http://localhost:8000/api/v1/posts/1
http://localhost:8000/api/v1/posts/1/comments
```

However, note that if we are having versions in our URI and routes, then it is better to keep that version actually applicable in our controllers as well. Without that, version implementation will be very limited. To do so, we should have a version-based namespace for controllers. In our controllers (both `PostController` and `CommentController`), namespace will be changed to the following line of code:

```
namespace App\Http\Controllers\V1;
```

Now, the controllers directory structure should match the namespace as well. So, let's create a directory named V1 in the `Controllers` directory and move our controllers inside the `app\Http\Controllers\`**V1** directory. When we will have the next version, we will make another directory named V2 in `app\Http\Controllers` and add new controllers in it. It will also result in a new namespace App\Http\Controllers**V2**. With a namespace and directory change, controller's paths in `routes/web.php` will also need to be changed accordingly.

With this change, you will most probably see the following error:

```
Class 'App\Http\Controllers\V1\Controller' not found
```

So, either move `Controller.php` in the controllers directory to the V1 directory or simply access it with a complete namespace such as `\App\Http\Controllers\Controller` as shown here:

```
class PostController extends \App\Http\Controllers\Controller
{..
```

It is up to you how you do it.

Rate limiting

Rate limiting is also known as throttling. It means that there should be a limit on how much time a particular client is able to hit the API endpoint in a specific time interval. To enable it, we must enable the `api.throttling` middleware. You can apply throttling on all routes or on specific routes. You will just apply middleware on that particular route as shown here. In our case, we want to enable it for all endpoints, so let's put it in a version group:

```
$api->version('v1', ['middleware' => 'api.throttle','prefix' => 'api/v1'],
function ($api) {
 $api->resource('posts', "App\Http\Controllers\V1\PostController");
 $api->resource('comments', "App\Http\Controllers\V1\CommentController", [
 'except' => ['store', 'index']
 ]);

$api->post('posts/{id}/comments',
 'App\Http\V1\Controllers\CommentController@store');
$api->get('posts/{id}/comments',
 'App\Http\V1\Controllers\CommentController@index');

});
```

Just for the sake of simplicity, let's make a change in routes. Instead of specifying namespace with every controller's name, we can simply use namespace in a version group as follows:

```
$api->version('v1', ['middleware' => 'api.throttle',
'prefix' => 'api/v1', namespace =>
"App\HttpControllers\V1" ]
```

Now, we can simply remove it from the controller path.

You can also mention the limit and time interval in minutes:

```
$api->version('v1', [
    'middleware' => 'api.throttle',
    'limit' => 100,
    'expires' => 5,
    'prefix' => 'api/v1',
    'namespace' => 'App\Http\Controllers\V1'
    ],
  function ($api) {
    $api->resource('posts', "PostController");
    $api->resource('comments', "CommentController", [
        'except' => ['store', 'index']
    ]);

    $api->post('posts/{id}/comments', 'CommentController@store');
    $api->get('posts/{id}/comments', 'CommentController@index');

});
```

Here, `expires` is the time interval, while `limit` is the number of times a route can be accessed.

Internal requests

We are mostly making an API to be accessed as a web service from the outside by an external client, not from the same application. However, sometimes, we are in a situation where we need to make internal requests within the same application and want data in the same format as it is being returned to external clients.

Let's say now you want comments data in `PostController` from the API as it returns a response instead of an internal function call. We want the same data that the `/api/posts/{postId}/comments` endpoint returns when hit from Postman or another client. In that case, the Dingo API package helps us. Here is how simple it is:

```
use Illuminate\Http\Request;
use Illuminate\Http\Response;
use Illuminate\Http\JsonResponse;
use Dingo\Api\Routing\Helpers;

class PostController extends Controller
{
    use Helpers;

    public function __construct(\App\Post $post)
    {
        $this->post = $post;
    }
....
/**
 * Display the specified resource.
 *
 * @param  int  $id
 * @return \Illuminate\Http\Response
 */
public function show($id)
{
 $comments = $this->api->get("api/posts/$id/comments");

 $post = $this->post->find($id);
....
 }
....
}
```

Bold statements in the preceding code snippet is what is different, and it contributes in making an internal request. As you can say, we have made a GET-based request to the endpoint:

```
$comments = $this->api->get("api/posts/$id/comments");
```

We can also make it a POST-based request by just using a different method as follows:

```
$this->api->post("api/v1/posts/$id/comments", ['comment' => 'a nice
post']);
```

Responses

The Dingo API package provides a lot more support for different types of responses. As we will not go in to the detail of each and every thing Dingo API provides, you can review it in its documentation at `https://github.com/dingo/api/wiki/Responses`.

However, later in this chapter, we will look at responses and formats in detail.

We will use the Dingo API package for other things as well, but for now, let's move towards other concepts and we will keep using the Dingo API package side by side.

Authentication and middleware

We have already discussed several times that for a RESTful web service, a session is maintained through an authentication token stored on the client side. So, the server can look for the authentication token and can find that user's session stored on the server.

There are several ways to generate a token. In our case, we will use **JWT (JSON Web Tokens)**. As told on `jwt.io`:

JSON Web Tokens are an open, industry standard RFC 7519 method for representing claims securely between two parties.

We will not go into complete detail about JWT as JWT is a way to transfer information between two parties (in our case, client and server) as JWT can be used for many purposes. Instead, we will use it for access/authentication tokens to maintain stateless sessions. So, we will stick with what we need from JWT. We need it for maintaining sessions for authentication purposes, and this is something the Dingo API package will also help us with.

In fact, Dingo API supports three authentication providers at the time of writing this book. By default, HTTP Basic Authentication is enabled. The other two are JWT Auth and OAuth 2.0. We will use JWT Auth.

JWT Auth setup

The package that Dingo API uses to integrate JWT authentication can be found at `https://github.com/tymondesigns/jwt-auth`.

There are two ways to set up JWT Auth:

1. We can simply follow instructions for the JWT Auth package and configure it to use with Dingo manually and fix problems one by one manually.
2. We can simply install another package that helps us install and set up Dingo API and JWT Auth together with some basic configurations.

Here, we will see both ways. However, with the manual way, it can be ambiguous because of different versions of different packages and Lumen itself. So, although I am going to show the manual way, I would recommend that you use an integration package so that you don't need to deal with every thing at a low level manually. I will show you the manual way just to give you some idea of what is included underneath.

The Manual way

Let's install the package as mentioned on the installation page at `https://github.com/tymondesigns/jwt-auth/wiki/Installation`.

First of all, we need to install the JWT Auth package:

```
composer require tymon/jwt-auth 1.0.0-beta.3
```

Note that this version is for Laravel 5.3. For older versions, you might need to use a different version of the JWT Auth package, most probably version 0.5.

To register the service provider in the `bootstrap/app.php` file, add this line of code:

```
$app->register(Tymon\JWTAuth\Providers\JWTAuthServiceProvider::class);
```

Then, add these two class aliases in the same `bootstrap/app.php` file:

```
class_alias('Tymon\JWTAuth\Facades\JWTAuth', 'JWTAuth');
class_alias('Tymon\JWTAuth\Facades\JWTFactory', 'JWTFactory');
```

Then, you need to generate a random key that will be used to sign our tokens. To do so, run this command:

```
php artisan jwt:generate
```

This will generate a random key.

You might see some error as shown here:

```
[Illuminate\Contracts\Container\BindingResolutionExceptio
n] Unresolvable dependency resolving [Parameter #0 [
<required> $app ]] in class Illuminate\Cache\CacheManager
```

In this case, add the following lines in bootstrap/app.php right after
$app->withEloquent();. So, it will fix the problem and you can try
generating a random key:

```
$app->alias('cache', 'Illuminate\Cache\CacheManager');
$app->alias('auth', 'Illuminate\Auth\AuthManager');
```

However, you are probably wondering where this random key will be set. Actually, some
packages were not built for Lumen and require a structure more like Laravel. The
tymondesigns/jwt-auth package is one of them. What it needs is a way to publish
configurations. While Lumen does not have separate configuration files for different
packages, as we need it, we can simply let Lumen have such a config file for this package.
To do so, if you don't have helpers.php under app/ directory, then create it and add the
following content:

```php
<?php
if ( ! function_exists('config_path'))
{
    /**
     * Get the configuration path.
     *
     * @param  string $path
     * @return string
     */
    function config_path($path = '')
    {
        return app()->basePath() . '/config' . ($path ? '/' . $path :
$path);
    }
}
```

Then, add `helpers.php` to `composer.json` in the auto-load array:

```
"autoload": {
  "psr-4": {
    "App\\": "app/"
  },
  "files": [
    "app/helpers.php"
  ]
},
```

Run the following command:

```
composer dump-autoload
```

Once you have it, run the following command:

```
php artisan vendor:publish --
provider="Tymon\JWTAuth\Providers\JWTAuthServiceProvider"
```

At this point, you will get another error saying:

```
[Symfony\Component\Console\Exception\CommandNotFoundException]
  There are no commands defined in the "vendor" namespace.
```

Don't worry; it is all expected. It is because Lumen does not have the `vendor:publish` command out of the box. So, we need to install a small package for this command:

```
composer require laravelista/lumen-vendor-publish
```

As this command is going to have a new command, in order to use that command, we need to put the following in the `$commands` array in `app/Console/Kernel.php`.

Now, try running the same command again as shown here:

```
php artisan vendor:publish --
provider="Tymon\JWTAuth\Providers\JWTAuthServiceProvider"
```

This time, you will see something like this:

```
Copied File [/vendor/tymon/jwt-auth/src/config/config.php] To
[/config/jwt.php]
Publishing complete for tag []!
```

Now, we have `blog/config/jwt.php` and we can store the `jwt-auth` package-related configurations in this file.

The first thing we need to do is to rerun this command to set random key sign signatures:

```
php artisan jwt:generate
```

This time, you can see this key set in the `config/jwt.php` file in the return array:

```
'secret' => env('JWT_SECRET', 'RusJ3fiLAp4DmUNNzqGpC7IcQI8bfar7'),
```

The next, you need to do configurations as shown in `https://github.com/tymondesigns/jwt-auth/wiki/Configuration`.

However, you can also keep other settings in `config/jwt.php` as default.

Next thing will be to tell Dingo API to use JWT as the authentication method. So add this in `bootstrap/app.php`:

```
app('Dingo\Api\Auth\Auth')->extend('jwt', function ($app) {
  return new Dingo\Api\Auth\Provider\JWT($app['Tymon\JWTAuth\JWTAuth']);
});
```

As per the JWT Auth documentation, we are mostly done with configurations, but note that you may face small issues related to versions. If you are using a version older than Lumen 5.3, then note that a different version of JWT Auth is required based on the different Laravel version. For version 5.2, you should use JWT Auth Version 0.5. So, if you still get any errors in the version older than Laravel 5.2, then note that it is possible that the error is because of version difference, so you have to search on the Internet.

As you can see, just to use two packages together to achieve some functionality, we have to spend some time on configurations, as suggested in the last few steps. Even then, there is a chance of errors because of version differences. So, an easy and simple way is to not install the Dingo API package and JWT Auth package manually. There is another package, installing which will install the Dingo API package, Lumen generators, **CORS** (**Cross Origin Resource Sharing**) support, and JWTAuth and make it available to use without that much configuration. Now, let's look at that.

Simpler way through Lumen JWT authentication integration package

An easier way is to install both Dingo API package and JWT Auth yourself is to simply install `https://packagist.org/packages/krisanalfa/lumen-dingo-adapter`.

It will add Dingo and JWT in your Lumen-based application. Simply install this package:

```
composer require krisanalfa/lumen-dingo-adapter
```

Then, in `bootstrap/app.php`, add the following lines of code:

```
$app->register(Zeek\LumenDingoAdapter\Providers\LumenDingoAdapterServicePro
vider::class);
```

Now, this way, we are using this `LumenDingoAdapter` package, so here is the `bootstrap/app.php` file that we will use so that you can compare it with yours:

```php
<?php

require_once __DIR__.'/../vendor/autoload.php';

try {
    (new Dotenv\Dotenv(__DIR__.'/../'))->load();
} catch (Dotenv\Exception\InvalidPathException $e) {
    //
}

/*
|--------------------------------------------------------------------------
| Create The Application
|--------------------------------------------------------------------------
|
| Here we will load the environment and create the application instance
| that serves as the central piece of this framework. We'll use this
| application as an "IoC" container and router for this framework.
|
*/

$app = new Laravel\Lumen\Application(
    realpath(__DIR__.'/../')
);


$app->withFacades();

$app->withEloquent();

/*
|--------------------------------------------------------------------------
| Register Container Bindings
|--------------------------------------------------------------------------
|
| Now we will register a few bindings in the service container. We will
| register the exception handler and the console kernel. You may add
| your own bindings here if you like or you can make another file.
|
*/
```

```
$app->singleton(
    Illuminate\Contracts\Debug\ExceptionHandler::class,
    App\Exceptions\Handler::class
);

$app->singleton(
    Illuminate\Contracts\Console\Kernel::class,
    App\Console\Kernel::class
);

$app->register(Zeek\LumenDingoAdapter\Providers\LumenDingoAdapterServicePro
vider::class);


/*
|--------------------------------------------------------------------------
| Register Middleware
|--------------------------------------------------------------------------
|
| Next, we will register the middleware with the application. These can
| be global middleware that run before and after each request into a
| route or middleware that'll be assigned to some specific routes.
|
*/

// $app->middleware([
//     App\Http\Middleware\ExampleMiddleware::class
// ]);

// $app->routeMiddleware([
//     'auth' => App\Http\Middleware\Authenticate::class,
// ]);

/*
|--------------------------------------------------------------------------
| Register Service Providers
|--------------------------------------------------------------------------
|
| Here we will register all of the application's service providers which
| are used to bind services into the container. Service providers are
| totally optional, so you are not required to uncomment this line.
|
*/

// $app->register(App\Providers\AppServiceProvider::class);
// $app->register(App\Providers\AuthServiceProvider::class);
// $app->register(App\Providers\EventServiceProvider::class);
```

```
/*
|------------------------------------------------------------------------
| Load The Application Routes
|------------------------------------------------------------------------
|
| Next we will include the routes file so that they can all be added to
| the application. This will provide all of the URLs the application
| can respond to, as well as the controllers that may handle them.
|
*/

$app->group(['namespace' => 'App\Http\Controllers'], function ($app) {
    require __DIR__.'/../routes/web.php';
});

return $app;
```

If you are wondering what exactly this `$app->withFacades()` do then note that this enables facades in application. Facades is a design pattern which is used to make complex things abstract while providing simplified interface to interact with. In Lumen, as told by Laravel documentation: *Facades provide a "static" interface to classes that are available in the application's service container.*

Benefit of using facades is that it provides memorable syntax. We are not going to use Facades frequently, and will try to avoid using it because we will favor dependency injection over it. However, some packages will may be using facades so to let them work, we have enabled facades.

Authentication

Now, we can protect our endpoints using the `api.auth` middleware. This middleware checks for user authentication and gets user from JWT. However, the first thing is to make the user log in, create a token based on that user information, and return the signed token to the client.

In order to have authentication working, we first need to create an authentication-related controller. That controller will not only do token creation based on user login, it will also make the user token expire and refresh the token. In order to do this, we can put this open source `AuthController` in the `app/Http/Controllers/Auth/` directory at `https://github.com/Haafiz/REST-API-for-basic-RPG/blob/master/app/Http/Controllers/Auth/AuthController.php`.

Just to give credit, I want to tell you that the version we are using for AuthController is a modified version of https://github.com/krisanalfa/lumen-jwt/blob/develop/app/Http/Controllers/Auth/AuthController.php.

Anyway, in case you don't see AuthController available online while reading the book, here is the content of AuthController:

```php
<?php

namespace App\Http\Controllers\Auth;

use Illuminate\Http\Request;
use Illuminate\Http\Response;
use Illuminate\Http\JsonResponse;
use Tymon\JWTAuth\Facades\JWTAuth;
use App\Http\Controllers\Controller;
use Tymon\JWTAuth\Exceptions\JWTException;
use Illuminate\Http\Exception\HttpResponseException;

class AuthController extends Controller
{
    /**
     * Handle a login request to the application.
     *
     * @param \Illuminate\Http\Request $request
     *
     * @return \Illuminate\Http\Response;
     */
    public function login(Request $request)
    {
        try {
            $this->validateLoginRequest($request);
        } catch (HttpResponseException $e) {
            return $this->onBadRequest();
        }

        try {
            // Attempt to verify the credentials and create a token for the
user
            if (!$token = JWTAuth::attempt(
                $this->getCredentials($request)
            )) {
                return $this->onUnauthorized();
            }
        } catch (JWTException $e) {
            // Something went wrong whilst attempting to encode the token
            return $this->onJwtGenerationError();
```

```
    }

    // All good so return the token
    return $this->onAuthorized($token);
}

/**
 * Validate authentication request.
 *
 * @param  Request $request
 * @return void
 * @throws HttpResponseException
 */
protected function validateLoginRequest(Request $request)
{
    $this->validate(
        $request, [
            'email' => 'required|email|max:255',
            'password' => 'required',
        ]
    );
}

/**
 * What response should be returned on bad request.
 *
 * @return JsonResponse
 */
protected function onBadRequest()
{
    return new JsonResponse(
        [
            'message' => 'invalid_credentials'
        ], Response::HTTP_BAD_REQUEST
    );
}

/**
 * What response should be returned on invalid credentials.
 *
 * @return JsonResponse
 */
protected function onUnauthorized()
{
    return new JsonResponse(
        [
            'message' => 'invalid_credentials'
        ], Response::HTTP_UNAUTHORIZED
```

```
        );
    }

    /**
     * What response should be returned on error while generate JWT.
     *
     * @return JsonResponse
     */
    protected function onJwtGenerationError()
    {
        return new JsonResponse(
            [
                'message' => 'could_not_create_token'
            ], Response::HTTP_INTERNAL_SERVER_ERROR
        );
    }

    /**
     * What response should be returned on authorized.
     *
     * @return JsonResponse
     */
    protected function onAuthorized($token)
    {
        return new JsonResponse(
            [
                'message' => 'token_generated',
                'data' => [
                    'token' => $token,
                ]
            ]
        );
    }

    /**
     * Get the needed authorization credentials from the request.
     *
     * @param \Illuminate\Http\Request $request
     *
     * @return array
     */
    protected function getCredentials(Request $request)
    {
        return $request->only('email', 'password');
    }

    /**
     * Invalidate a token.
```

```php
     *
     * @return \Illuminate\Http\Response
     */
    public function invalidateToken()
    {
        $token = JWTAuth::parseToken();

        $token->invalidate();

        return new JsonResponse(['message' => 'token_invalidated']);
    }

    /**
     * Refresh a token.
     *
     * @return \Illuminate\Http\Response
     */
    public function refreshToken()
    {
        $token = JWTAuth::parseToken();

        $newToken = $token->refresh();

        return new JsonResponse(
            [
                'message' => 'token_refreshed',
                'data' => [
                    'token' => $newToken
                ]
            ]
        );
    }

    /**
     * Get authenticated user.
     *
     * @return \Illuminate\Http\Response
     */
    public function getUser()
    {
        return new JsonResponse(
            [
                'message' => 'authenticated_user',
                'data' => JWTAuth::parseToken()->authenticate()
            ]
        );
    }
}
```

This controller does three major tasks:

- Login in `login()` method
- Invalidate token
- Refresh token

Log in

Log in is being done in the `login()` method, and it tries to log in using `JWTAuth::attempt($this->getCredentials($request))`. If credentials are not valid or if there is some other problem, it will just return an error. However, to access this `login()` method, we need to add a route for it. Here is what we will add in `routes/web.php`:

```
$api->post(
    '/auth/login', [
        'as' => 'api.auth.login',
        'uses' => 'Auth\AuthController@login',
    ]
);
```

Invalidate token

To invalidate token, in other words, to log out user, the `invalidateToken()` method will be used. This method will be called through a route. We will add the following route with the delete request method, which will call `AuthController::invalidateToken()` from the routed file:

```
$api->delete(
    '/', [
        'uses' => 'Auth/AuthController@invalidateToken',
        'as' => 'api.auth.invalidate'
    ]
);
```

Refresh token

Refresh token is called when the token has expired based on the expiry time. In order to refresh the token, we also need to add the following route:

```
$api->patch(
    '/', [
        'uses' => 'Auth/AuthController@refreshToken',
        'as' => 'api.auth.refresh'
    ]
);
```

Note that all these endpoints will be added under version v1.

Once we have this `AuthController` there and routes are set up, the user can log in using the following endpoint:

```
POST /api/v1/auth/login
Params: email, passsword
```

Try this and you will get a JWT-based access token.

Lumen, Dingo, JWT Auth, and CORS boilerplate:

If you face difficulty in configuring Lumen with Dingo and JWT, then you can simply use the repository at `https://github.com/krisanalfa/lumen-jwt`.

This repository will provide you with boilerplate code for setting up your Lumen for API development using Dingo API and JWT. You can clone this and simply start using it. It is nothing other than a Lumen integration with JWT, Dingo API, and CORS support. So, if you are starting a new RESTful web services project, you can simply start with this boiler plate code.

Before proceeding, let's look at our routes file to make sure we are on the same page:

```php
<?php

/*
|--------------------------------------------------------------------------
| Application Routes
|--------------------------------------------------------------------------
|
| Here is where you can register all of the routes for an application.
```

```
| It is a breeze. Simply tell Lumen the URIs it should respond to
| and give it the Closure to call when that URI is requested.
|
*/
$api = app('Dingo\Api\Routing\Router');


$api->version('v1', [
    'middleware' => ['api.throttle'],
    'limit' => 100,
    'expires' => 5,
    'prefix' => 'api/v1',
    'namespace' => 'App\Http\Controllers\V1'
],
    function ($api) {
        $api->group(['middleware' => 'api.auth'], function ($api) {
            //Posts protected routes
            $api->resource('posts', "PostController", [
                'except' => ['show', 'index']
            ]);

            //Comments protected routes
            $api->resource('comments', "CommentController", [
                'except' => ['show', 'index']
            ]);

            $api->post('posts/{id}/comments', 'CommentController@store');


            // Logout user by removing token
            $api->delete(
                '/', [
                    'uses' => 'Auth/AuthController@invalidateToken',
                    'as' => 'api.Auth.invalidate'
                ]
            );


            // Refresh token
            $api->patch(
                '/', [
                    'uses' => 'Auth/AuthController@refreshToken',
                    'as' => 'api.Auth.refresh'
                ]
            );
        });

    $api->get('posts', 'PostController@index');
```

```
$api->get('posts/{id}', 'PostController@show');

$api->get('posts/{id}/comments', 'CommentController@index');
$api->get('comments/{id}', 'CommentController@show');

$api->post(
'/auth/login', [
'as' => 'api.Auth.login',
'uses' => 'Auth\AuthController@login',
]
);
});

$app->get('/', function () use ($app) {
 return $app->version();
});
```

As you can see, we have made a route group. A route group is just a way to group similar routes in which we can apply the same middleware or namespace or prefix and so on, just like we did in the v1 group.

Here, we made another route group so that we can add the api.auth middleware on it. Another thing to note is that we have split some posts routes from post resource route to separate routes just to have some routes available without login. We did the same for comments routes as well.

 Note that if you don't want to split some routes from the resource route, then you can do that as well. You will just add the api.auth middleware in controllers instead of routes file. Both ways are correct; it is just a matter of preference. I did it this way because I find it easier to know which routes are protected from the same routes file instead of constructors of different controllers. But again, it is up to you.

We are letting only logged in users create, update, and delete posts. However, we need to make sure that the user that is logged in can only update or delete their own posts. Although this thing can also be done by creating another middleware, it will be simpler to do it in controller.

This is how we do it in PostController:

```
<?php

namespace App\Http\Controllers\V1;

use Illuminate\Http\Request;
```

```
use Illuminate\Http\Response;
use Illuminate\Http\JsonResponse;
use Tymon\JWTAuth\Facades\JWTAuth;
use Dingo\Api\Routing\Helpers;

class PostController extends Controller
{
    use Helpers;

    public function __construct(\App\Post $post)
    {

        $this->post = $post;

    }

    /**
     * Display a listing of the resource.
     *
     * @return \Illuminate\Http\Response
     */
    public function index(Request $request)
    {
        $posts = $this->post->paginate(20);

        return $posts;
    }

    /**
     * Store a newly created resource in storage.
     *
     * @param  \Illuminate\Http\Request  $request
     * @return \Illuminate\Http\Response
     */
    public function store(Request $request)
    {

        $input = $request->all();
        $input['user_id'] = $this->user->id;

        $validationRules = [
            'content' => 'required|min:1',
            'title' => 'required|min:1',
            'status' => 'required|in:draft,published',
            'user_id' => 'required|exists:users,id'
        ];

        $validator = \Validator::make($input, $validationRules);
```

```php
    if ($validator->fails()) {
        return new JsonResponse(
            [
                'errors' => $validator->errors()
            ], Response::HTTP_BAD_REQUEST
        );
    }

    $this->post->create($input);

    return [
        'data' => $input
    ];
}

/**
 * Display the specified resource.
 *
 * @param  int  $id
 * @return \Illuminate\Http\Response
 */
public function show($id)
{
    $post = $this->post->find($id);

    if(!$post) {
        abort(404);
    }

    return $post;
}

/**
 * Update the specified resource in storage.
 *
 * @param  \Illuminate\Http\Request  $request
 * @param  int  $id
 * @return \Illuminate\Http\Response
 */
public function update(Request $request, $id)
{
    $input = $request->all();

    $post = $this->post->find($id);

    if(!$post) {
        abort(404);
    }
```

```php
        if($this->user->id != $post->user_id){
            return new JsonResponse(
                [
                    'errors' => 'Only Post Owner can update it'
                ], Response::HTTP_FORBIDDEN
            );
        }

        $post->fill($input);
        $post->save();

        return $post;
    }

    /**
     * Remove the specified resource from storage.
     *
     * @param  int  $id
     * @return \Illuminate\Http\Response
     */
    public function destroy($id)
    {
        $post = $this->post->find($id);

        if(!$post) {
            abort(404);
        }

        if($this->user->id != $post->user_id){
            return new JsonResponse(
                [
                    'errors' => 'Only Post Owner can delete it'
                ], Response::HTTP_FORBIDDEN
            );
        }

        $post->delete();

        return ['message' => 'deleted successfully', 'post_id' => $id];
    }
}
```

As you can see, there are three places where I have highlighted code. In the `store()` method, we got the user ID from it and put it in the input array so that the `user_id` of post will be based on the token. Similarly, for `update()` and `delete()`, we used that user's ID and placed a check to make sure that Post owner is deleting or updating post records. You are probably wondering that when we haven't defined the `$this->user` property anywhere, how are we accessing it? Actually, we are using the Helpers trait, so `$this->user` is coming from that trait.

 Note that in order to access protected resources, you should grab the token from the login endpoint and put it in your header as follows:
`Authentication: bearer <token grabbed from login>`

In the same way, `CommentController` will have checks to make sure that comments modification will be limited to the comment owner only and deletion will be limited to the comment or post owner. It will have similar checks and user ID through token in the same way. So, I will leave that to you to implement comment controller to have those checks.

Transformers

In full-stack MVC framework, we have Model View Controller. In Lumen or in API, we don't have Views because we just return some data. However, we may want to show data in a different way than usual. We may want to use a different format, or we may want to restrict an object with a specific format. In all such cases, we need a place where formatting-related tasks will be done, a place where we can have different format-related content. We can have it in controller. However, we will need to define the same format at different places. In that case, we can add a method in model. For example, post model can have a specific way to format a post object. So, we can define another method in Post Model.

It will work fine, but if you look at it closely, it is related to formatting, not model. So, we have another layer called serializes or transformers. Also, sometimes, we need nested objects, so we will not want to do the same nesting again and again.

Lumen provides a way to serialize data to JSON. In Eloquent object, there is a method named `toJson()`; this method can be overridden to serve the purpose. However, it is better to have a separate layer for formatting and serializing data than having just a method to do so in the same class. Then comes transformers; a transformer is just another layer. You can think of a transformer as the View layer of an API or web service.

Understanding and setting transformers

Actually, the package we used, named, Dingo API, contains a lot of stuff that we need to create a RESTful web service. The same Dingo API package provides support for transformers as well.

Before doing anything, we need to understand that the transformer layer consists of transformers. A transformer is a class responsible for data presentation. Dingo API transformers support transformers, and for transformers, the API depends on another library responsible for transformer functionality. It is up to us which transformation layer or library we use. By default, it comes with Fractal, a default transformation layer.

We don't need to do anything else related to setup. Let's move towards using transformer for our objects. However, before that, make yourself comfortable with Fractal. We need to at least know what Fractal is and what it provides. The documentation for Fractal can be found at `http://fractal.thephpleague.com/`.

Using transformers

There are two ways to tell Lumen which transformer class has to be used. For that, we need to create a transformer class. Let's first make a transformer for our `Post` object and name it `PostTransformer`. First, create a directory named `app/Transformers` and in that directory, create a class `PostTransformer` with the following content:

```php
<?php

namespace App\Transformers;

use League\Fractal;

class PostTransformer extends Fractal\TransformerAbstract
{
    public function transform(\App\Post $post)
    {
        return $post->toArray();
```

```
    }
}
```

You can do whatever you want to do with the Post response in the `transform()` method.
Note that we are not optionally overriding the `transform()` method here, but we are
providing an implementation of `transform()`. You always need to add that method in the
transformer class. However, this class is of no use if it is not used from anywhere. So, let's
use it from our `PostController`. Let's do it in the `index()` method:

```
public function index(\App\Transformers\PostTransformer $postTransformer)
{
    $posts = $this->post->paginate(20);

    return $this->response->paginator($posts, $postTransformer);
}
```

As you can see, we have injected the `PostTransformer` object to the
`$this->response->paginator()` method. The first thing we need to note here is the
`$this->response->paginator()` method and the `$this->response` object. We now
need to know from where the `$this->response` object came from in the first place. We got
it because we used the `Helpers` trait in `PostController`. Anyway, now, let's see how it
works. Hit the `PostController` `index()` method with the following endpoint:

```
http://localhost:8000/api/v1/posts
```

It will return something like this:

```
{
"data": [
    {
        "id": 1,
        "title": "test",
        "status": "draft",
        "content": "test post",
        "user_id": 2,
        "created_at": null,
        "updated_at": "2017-06-28 00:47:50"
    },
    {
        "id": 3,
        "title": "test",
        "status": "published",
        "content": "test post",
        "user_id": 2,
        "created_at": "2017-06-28 00:00:44",
        "updated_at": "2017-06-28 00:00:44"
```

```
        },
        {
            "id": 4,
            "title": "test",
            "status": "published",
            "content": "test post",
            "user_id": 2,
            "created_at": "2017-06-28 03:21:36",
            "updated_at": "2017-06-28 03:21:36"
        },
        {
            "id": 5,
            "title": "test post",
            "status": "draft",
            "content": "This is yet another post for testing purpose",
            "user_id": 8,
            "created_at": "2017-07-15 00:45:29",
            "updated_at": "2017-07-15 00:45:29"
        },
        {
            "id": 6,
            "title": "test post",
            "status": "draft",
            "content": "This is yet another post for testing purpose",
            "user_id": 8,
            "created_at": "2017-07-15 23:53:23",
            "updated_at": "2017-07-15 23:53:23"
        }
    ],
    "meta": {
        "pagination": {
            "total": 5,
            "count": 5,
            "per_page": 20,
            "current_page": 1,
            "total_pages": 1,
            "links": []
        }
    }
}
```

If you look at it, you will see a separate meta section having pagination-related content. This is a small thing that Fractal transformer provides by itself. Actually, there is a lot more that Fractal can do for us.

We can include nested objects. For example, if we have `user_id` in `Post` and we want the `User` object nested inside the same `Post` object, then it can provide an easier way to do that as well. Although the transformer layer is just like the view layer for API response data, it provides a lot more than that. Right now, I will show you how our `PostController` method will look after returning with `PostTransformer` from `show()` and other methods. For details of Fractal, I would recommend that you look at the Fractal documentation, so that you can take full advantage of it, at `http://fractal.thephpleague.com/`.

Here is how our `PostController` method will look:

```php
<?php

namespace App\Http\Controllers\V1;

use Illuminate\Http\Request;
use Illuminate\Http\Response;
use Illuminate\Http\JsonResponse;
use Dingo\Api\Routing\Helpers;
use App\Transformers\PostTransformer;

class PostController extends Controller
{
    use Helpers;

    public function __construct(\App\Post $post,
\App\Transformers\PostTransformer $postTransformer)
    {
        $this->post = $post;

        $this->transformer = $postTransformer;

    }

    /**
     * Display a listing of the resource.
     *
     * @return \Illuminate\Http\Response
     */
    public function index()
    {
        $posts = $this->post->paginate(20);

        return $this->response->paginator($posts, $this->transformer);
    }

    /**
     * Store a newly created resource in storage.
```

```
 *
 * @param  \Illuminate\Http\Request  $request
 * @return \Illuminate\Http\Response
 */
public function store(Request $request)
{

    $input = $request->all();
    $input['user_id'] = $this->user->id;

    $validationRules = [
        'content' => 'required|min:1',
        'title' => 'required|min:1',
        'status' => 'required|in:draft,published',
        'user_id' => 'required|exists:users,id'
    ];

    $validator = \Validator::make($input, $validationRules);
    if ($validator->fails()) {
        return new JsonResponse(
            [
                'errors' => $validator->errors()
            ], Response::HTTP_BAD_REQUEST
        );
    }

    $post = $this->post->create($input);

    return $this->response->item($post, $this->transformer);
}

/**
 * Display the specified resource.
 *
 * @param  int  $id
 * @return \Illuminate\Http\Response
 */
public function show($id)
{
    $post = $this->post->find($id);

    if(!$post) {
        abort(404);
    }

    return $this->response->item($post, $this->transformer);
}
```

```
/**
 * Update the specified resource in storage.
 *
 * @param  \Illuminate\Http\Request  $request
 * @param  int  $id
 * @return \Illuminate\Http\Response
 */
public function update(Request $request, $id)
{
    $input = $request->all();

    $post = $this->post->find($id);

    if(!$post) {
        abort(404);
    }

    if($this->user->id != $post->user_id){
        return new JsonResponse(
            [
                'errors' => 'Only Post Owner can update it'
            ], Response::HTTP_FORBIDDEN
        );
    }

    $post->fill($input);
    $post->save();

    return $this->response->item($post, $this->transformer);
}

/**
 * Remove the specified resource from storage.
 *
 * @param  int  $id
 * @return \Illuminate\Http\Response
 */
public function destroy($id)
{
    $post = $this->post->find($id);

    if(!$post) {
        abort(404);
    }

    if($this->user->id != $post->user_id){
        return new JsonResponse(
            [
```

```
                            'errors' => 'Only Post Owner can delete it'
                    ], Response::HTTP_FORBIDDEN
            );
        }

        $post->delete();

        return ['message' => 'deleted successfully', 'post_id' => $id];
    }
}
```

From the highlighted lines in the preceding code snippet, you can see that we have added the `PostTransformer` object in constructor and placed it in `$this->transformer` that we used in other methods. Another thing you can see is that at one place, we used the `$this->response->paginator()` method in the `index()` method, while we used `$this->response->item()` in others. It is because `$this->response->item()` method is used when there is one object, while `paginator` is used when we have the `paginator` object in the `index()` method. Note that if you have a collection and do not have the `paginator` object, you should use `$this->response->collection()`.

As mentioned earlier, Fractal has more features and those are in its documentation. So, you need to take a pause and explore its documentation at `http://fractal.thephpleague.com/`.

Encryption

The next thing that we are missing is encryption of communication between client and server so that nobody can sniff and read data over the network. For this purpose, we will use **SSL** (**Secure Socket Layer**). As this book is not about encryption or cryptography or server setup, we will not go into the details of these concepts, but it is important that we talk about encryption here. If someone is able to sniff data over the network, then our website or web service is not secure.

In order to secure our web service, we will use HTTPS instead of HTTP. The "S" in HTTPS stands for Secure. Now, the question is how we can make it secure. Probably, you would say that we will use SSL as we said earlier. So what is SSL? SSL is Secure Socket Layer, a standard way to secure communication between server and browser. SSL refers to a security protocol. Actually SSL protocol had three versions, and they were insecure against some attacks. So what we actually use is **TLS** (**Transport Layer Security**). However, we still use SSL term when we are referring to TLS. If you want to use SSL certificate and SSL to make HTTP secure, actually what is used underneath is TLS which is better than original SSL protocols.

What happens is that when a connection is made, the server sends the SSL certificate's copy to the browser with the public key as well so that the browser can also encode or decode what is communicated to and from the server. We will not go into encryption details; however, we need to know how to get the SSL certificate.

SSL certificate, different options

Normally, the SSL certificate is bought from certificate providers. However, you can also get a free certificate from `letsencrypt.org`. So, if a free certificate is available, then why are certificates still bought? Actually, sometimes, buying it from some authorities is more about insurance than security. If you are making an e-commerce site or something that is accepting payment or very critical data such as financial information, then you need someone to take responsibility in front of your site's user.

Probably there is some minor difference (that I am unaware of) between a certificate from `letsencrypt.org` and from providers who sell for good prices, but normally, it is bought for insurance instead of security.

You will get installation instructions from whoever you get certificates from. If you prefer to go with `letsencrypt.org`, then I would recommend that you use certbot. Follow the instructions at `https://certbot.eff.org/`.

Summary

In this chapter, we discussed what we were missing in the previous chapter where we implemented RESTful web service endpoints in Lumen. We discussed throttling (Request Rate Limiting) to prevent DoS or brute force. We also implemented token-based authentication using some packages. Note that we only secured endpoints here, which we didn't want to leave accessible without user login. If there are other endpoints that you don't want to have public access to but they don't need users to log in, then you can use either some sort of key or basic authentication on those endpoints.

Other than that, we discussed and used transformers that are a sort of view layer for web services. Then, we briefly discussed encryption and SSL importance and then discussed the available options for SSL certificates.

In this chapter, I will not give you a list or URLs for more resources because we discussed a lot of different things in this chapter, so we were not able to go into the details of each and every thing. To completely absorb it, you should first look at the documentation of every thing that we discussed here, and then, you should practice. You will actually learn when you face problems during practice and when you attempt to solve them.

In the next chapter, we will talk about testing and write test cases for our endpoints and our code using automated testing tools.

8
API Testing – Guards on the Gates

In the last chapter, we fixed the issues that we had identified and completed the remaining things in our RESTful web service. However, to ensure quality we need to test our endpoints, and manual testing is not enough. In real-world projects, we can't test each endpoint repeatedly because in the real world there are a lot more endpoints. So, we move towards automated testing. We write test cases and execute them in an automated way. In fact, it makes more sense to write test cases first, run them, and then write code to fulfill the requirements of that test. This method of development is called **TDD** (**Test-driven Development**).

TDD is good and ensures that we are working exactly according to our test cases. However, in this book, we didn't use TDD because there were a lot of things to understand and we didn't want to include one more thing at the same time. So now, when we are done with the concepts, understanding, and writing the RESTful web service in Lumen (which was also new for many of us), now we can do this missing thing, that is, testing. TDD is not essential, but testing is. If we haven't written tests till now in favor of understanding other stuff, then we should do it now. The following are the topics that we will cover in this chapter:

- The need for automated API tests
- Types of tests:
    - Unit testing
    - Integration testing
    - Functional testing
    - Acceptance testing

- What type of tests will we write?
- Testing frameworks:
  - Introduction to CodeCeption
  - Setup and configurations
  - Writing API tests
  - Summary and more resources

The need for automated tests

As we discussed earlier, in the real world, we can't test every endpoint repeatedly after every major feature or change. We can try but we are human and we can miss out on that. The bigger problem is that we may sometimes think that we tested it but miss it and because there is no record of what we tested, we can't know. If we have a separate quality assurance team or person, they will most probably test and keep a record of that. However, in case of a RESTful web service, it will take more of their time or the possibility is that the QA person will test the end product as a whole and not RESTful web service.

Just like the RESTful web service works as one component or one side of a product, there are more low-level components of the RESTful web service as well. Not just endpoints but those endpoints depends on more low-level code. So in order to make our debugging easier, we write tests for these low-level components as well. Also, this way we can ensure that these low-level components are working fine and doing what they intend to. In case of any issues, we can run tests and know exactly what is not working properly.

Although, writing tests takes time at first but it is good in the long run. First of all, it saves the time of testing the same endpoints repeatedly after every change. Then, it helps a lot in case of refactoring something. It lets us know where the ripple effect is and what is affected because of our refactoring. Although, it takes time initially to write tests but it's worth it if we intend to make something that will remain there. In fact, the software development cost is less than the maintenance cost. This is because it will be developed once but to maintain and do the changes, it will consume more time. So, if we have written automated tests, it will ensure that everything is working exactly as required because the person who is maintaining the code is probably not the one who wrote it the first time.

There is no one type of testing that provides all these benefits but there are different types of testing, with each having their own benefits. Now that we know the importance of automated testing and writing test cases, let's learn about the different types of testing.

Types of testing

There are different types of testing in different contexts. In our case, we will discuss four major types of automated testing. These are the different types, based on how and what we test:

- Unit testing
- Integration testing
- Functional testing
- Acceptance testing

Unit testing

In unit testing, we test different units separately. By unit, we mean very small independent components. Obviously, components depend on each other but we consider a very small unit. In our case that small unit is class. The class is a unit that should have a single responsibility and it should be abstract from others and depend on the minimum number of other classes or components. Anyway, we can say in unit testing, we test class by creating an object of that class irrespective of whether it fulfills the required behavior.

One important thing to understand is that during unit tests, our test shouldn't touch code other than class/code under testing. If this code is interacting with some other object or external stuff during unit testing, we should mock these objects instead of interacting with actual objects so that the result of other object's methods should not affect the result of the unit/class we are testing. You are probably wondering what do we mean by mocking? **Mocking** means providing a fake object and setting it as per the desired behavior.

For example, if we are testing using the `User` class and it depends on the `Role` class, then a problem in the `Role` class shouldn't let the `User` class test fail. To achieve that, we will mock the `Role` object and inject in the `User` class object and then set the fixed return value for the method of the `Role` class that the `User` class is using. So next, it will actually invoke the `Role` class and will not depend on it.

The benefits of unit testing:

- It will let us know if a class is not doing what it intends to do. After some time, when the project is in maintenance, another developer will be able to understand what this class intends to do. What its methods are intended to do. So it will be like a manual of class written by a developer who knew why they wrote that class.

- Also, as we just discussed we should mock objects, on which class under testing depends, we should be able to inject the mocked object inside the object of the class under testing. If we will be able to do that and are able to manage without invoking an outside object, only then we can call our code, a testable code. If our code is not testable, then we cannot write a unit test for it. So, unit testing helps us make our code testable which actually is more loosely coupled code. So having the testable code is an advantage (as it is loosely coupled and more maintainable), even if we are not writing tests.
- It will let us debug where exactly the problem is if we are having any problems.
- As unit tests don't interact with outside objects, they are faster than some other types of testing.

 Developers who write unit tests are considered to be better developers, as code with tests is consider cleaner code because the developer has ensured that unit level components are not tightly coupled. And units tests can be used as a manual to what a class provides and how to use it.

Acceptance testing

Acceptance testing is the complete opposite of unit testing. Unit testing is done at the lowest level while acceptance testing is done at the highest level. Acceptance testing is how an end-user will see the product and how an end-user will interact with it. In case of a website, in acceptance testing, we write the test that hits the URL from outside. Testing tools simulate a browser or external client to hit the URL. In fact, some testing tools also provide an option to use a web browser, such as Chrome or Firefox.

 Most of the time, these tests are written by a QA team. It is because they are the people who are there to ensure that system is working for the end user, exactly how it is intended to. Also, these tests execution is slow. And for user interfaces, sometimes there is a lot of detail to test so a separate QA team does this type of testing. However, it is just a common practice, so there can be an exception to that depending on the situation.

The benefits of acceptance testing:

- Acceptance testing lets you see how an end user will see and interact with your software from outside
- It also lets you catch the problem, that will occur in any specific web browser because it uses a real web browser to execute tests

- As acceptance tests are written to be performed from outside, it doesn't matter which system you are testing and what technology or framework is used to write the system

For example, if you are writing test cases using a tool written in PHP, then you can use it for systems written in other languages as well. So it doesn't matter if development language is PHP, Python, Golang, or .Net. It is because acceptance tests hit the system from outside without any internal knowledge of the system. And it is the only one of these four types of tests which test the system without considering any inner detail.

Acceptance tests are very useful as they interact with your system with a real browser. So if some thing will not work in the specific browser, then these things can be identified. But keep in mind that with a real browser, these tests take time to execute. It is also slow if the browser simulation is used but still the browser simulation will take less time than the real browser. Note that acceptance testing is considered the slowest and most time consuming among these four types of tests.

Functional testing

Functional testing is similar to acceptance testing; however, it is from a different aspect. Functional testing is about testing functional requirements. It tests functional requirements and tests from outside the system. However, it has visibility inside and it can execute some code of the system in the test case.

Similar to acceptance testing it hits the URL; however, even to hit the URL, it executes code the browser or external client will execute on that specific the URL. However, it doesn't actually hit the URL from outside. Tests don't hit URL in reality, they just simulate it. It is because unlike acceptance testing, we are not interested in how exactly an end user will interact with it, instead if code is executed from that URL then we want to know the response.

We are more interested in if our functional requirements are met, and if not met then where is the problem?

The benefits of functional testing:

- With functional testing, the testing tool has access to the system, so it shows better error detail than acceptance testing.
- Functional tests don't actually open the browser or external client, so they are faster.

- In functional tests, we can also execute system code directly through the testing tool, so in some cases, we can do so to either save test case writing time, or to make test case execution faster. There are many testing tools available for that. We will use one of them named CodeCeption shortly.

Integration testing

Integration testing is very similar to unit testing in a way that in both types of testing we test classes by making their objects invoke their methods. But they are different in how we test classes. In case of unit testing, we don't touch other objects with which our class under test is interacting with. But in integration testing, we want to see how it all works together. We let them interact with each other.

Sometimes, everything is working fine as per the unit test but not at higher-level tests (functional test or acceptance test) where we test it on the basis of requirements by hitting the URL. So, in some cases, higher-level tests are failing and unit tests are passing so to narrow down where the problem is, integration tests are very useful. So, you can consider that the integration test stands somewhere between functional tests and unit tests. Functional testing is about testing the functional requirement while unit testing is about testing a single unit. So, an integration test is in the middle of both, it tests how these single units work together; however, it tests by testing small components from code but lets them interact with each other as well.

Some developers write integration tests and call it a unit test. Actually, integration tests just let code under the test to interact with other objects, so it can test how those classes work when they interact with system components. So, some people write integration tests if the code under test is very simple that needs to be tested while interacting with the system. However, it is not necessary to only write one unit test or integration test, you can write both if you have time.

The benefits of integration testing:

- Integration testing is useful when unit tests are not enough to catch bugs and high-level tests keep telling you that there is something wrong. So, integration tests helps in debugging the problem.
- Because of the nature of integration testing, it helps a lot in case of refactoring while telling you exactly what is affected by the new change.

What type of testing will we do?

Every type of testing has its own importance, especially unit testing. However, we will mainly do API testing that will be testing our RESTful web service endpoints. It never means that unit testing is less important, it is just that we are mainly focusing on API testing in this chapter because the book is focused on RESTful web services. In fact, testing is a big topic and you will be able to see complete books written on testing and TDD.

 Nowadays, **BDD (Behavior-driven Development)** is a more popular term. It is not completely different than TDD. It is just a different way of stating test cases. In fact, in BDD, there are no test cases instead there are specs. They serve the same purpose but BDD has a more friendly way to address the problem that is by stating specs and implementing them and that's how TDD works. So TDD and BDD are not different, just a different way to address the same problem.

We can perform API testing in both functional and acceptance testing ways. However, it makes more sense to write API tests as functional tests. Because functional tests will be fast as well as having an insight to our code base. It also makes more sense because acceptance tests are for end users and end users don't use API. The end user uses a user interface.

Testing frameworks

Just like we have frameworks for writing software, we have frameworks for writing test cases as well. As we are PHP developers, we will use a testing framework that is written in PHP or in which we can write test cases in PHP so that we can use it easily.

First of all, there are different testing frameworks that we can use in PHP, no matter which development framework we are using for application development. However, there are also testing tools that come with Laravel and Lumen. We can also use them for writing test cases. In fact, it will be easier to write test cases for Lumen but it will be Lumen and Laravel specific. Here, we will use a framework that you will be able to use outside the Lumen and Laravel ecosystems as well as for any PHP project, no matter which development framework you are using to write the code.

There are many different testing frameworks in PHP so how will we decide which one we want to use? We are going to use a framework that will not be so low level that we need to write everything by ourselves because we are not going to write unit tests but functional tests so we are picking up a bit of a high-level framework. A famous framework for unit testing is PHPUnit: `https://phpunit.de/`.

There is another unit testing framework in **BDD (Behavior-driven Development)** style named as PHPSpec: `http://www.phpspec.net` and PHPSpec is awesome if you are trying to learn or write unit tests. However, here we will be using a framework that is good for both functional and unit tests. Although, we are not writing unit tests but we want to consider a framework that you can later use for unit testing as well. The framework I have picked is CodeCeption: `http://codeception.com/` because it seems very good at API testing. Another BDD-style alternative could be Behat: `http://behat.org/en/latest/`. It is a high-level testing framework but it is better if we are doing acceptance testing or even better if we have a separate QA team who will be writing many test cases in the Gherkin syntax (`https://github.com/cucumber/cucumber/wiki/Gherkin`) that is very close to the natural language. However, Behat and Gherkin may have a bit more of a learning curve for PHP developers while CodeCeption is simply PHP (although it can use Gherkin if required), so as many readers will be new to writing test cases I will keep things simple and close to PHP. However, here is a detailed comparison I wrote 2 years ago on which framework to use for API testing, it is old but still valid for most of the stuff. If you are interested then you can have a look at `http://haafiz.me/programming/api-testing-selecting-testing-framework`.

CodeCeption introduction

CodeCeption is written in PHP and it is powered by PHPUnit. CodeCeption claims that *CodeCeption uses PHPUnit as a backend for running its tests. Thus, any PHPUnit test can be added to a CodeCeption test suite and then executed.*

Tests other than acceptance tests require a testing framework that has some insight or connection with code under the test. If we are using a development framework than a testing framework should has some sort of module or plugin for that framework. CodeCeption is good at this. It provides modules for different frameworks and CMS, such as Symfony, Joomla, Laravel, Lumen, Yii2, WordPress, and Zend frameworks. Just to let you know, these are just a few frameworks. CodeCeption has support for many other modules that can be helpful in different cases.

Setup and understanding the structure

There are different ways to install CodeCeption but I prefer composer and it is a standard way to install different PHP tools as PHP packages. So let's install that:

```
composer require "codeception/codeception" --dev
```

As you can see, we are using the `--dev` flag so that it will add CodeCeption in the `require-dev` block in the `composer.json` file. So, in production it will not be installed when you run `composer install --no-dev`, it will not install dependencies in the `require-dev` block. In case of confusion, check the composer-related chapter that is `Chapter 5`, *Load and resolve with Composer, an Evolutionary*.

After installing it, we need to set it up for writing test cases and to make it a part of our project. Installation just means that it is now in the `vendors` directory and now we can execute CodeCeption commands through composer.

To set up, we need to run the CodeCeption bootstrap command:

```
composer exec codecept bootstrap
```

`codecept` is CodeCeption's executable in the `vendor/bin` directory, so we executed it through composer and gave it an argument to run the `bootstrap` command. So after executing this command, some files and directories will be added in your project.

Here is a list of them:

```
codeception.yml

tests/_data/
tests/_output/

tests/acceptance/
tests/acceptance.suite.yml
tests/_support/AcceptanceTester.php
tests/_support/Helper/Acceptance.php
tests/_support/_generated/AcceptanceTesterActions.php

tests/functional/
tests/functional.suite.yml
tests/_support/FunctionalTester.php
tests/_support/Helper/Functional.php
tests/_support/_generated/FunctionalTesterActions.php

tests/unit/
tests/unit.suite.yml
tests/_support/UnitTester.php
tests/_support/Helper/Unit.php
tests/_support/_generated/UnitTesterActions.php
```

If you look at the mentioned list of files, then you will notice that we have one file at root, that is, `codeception.yml`, which contains the basic configurations of CodeCeption tests. It tells us about paths and basic settings. If you read this file, you will be able to easily understand it. If you don't understand something, ignore it for now. Other than this file, everything is in the `tests/` directory. This stuff is more important to us.

First of all, there are two empty directories in the `tests/` directory. `_output` contains output of test cases in case of failure and `_data` contains database queries in case we want to set up a default database for testing before and after running tests.

Other than that, you can see there are three groups of files having similar files with the difference of testing type. In CodeCeption, we know these groups as test suites. So, by default CodeCeption comes with three test suites. The acceptance, functional, and unit suites. All these three suites contain four files and one empty directory. So, let's look into the purpose of each of these files and directory.

tests/{suite-name}/

Here, `{suite-name}` will be replaced by the suite's actual name; like in case of unit suite, it will be `tests/unit/`.

Anyway, this directory will be used to save test cases that we will write.

tests/{suite-name}.suite.yml

This file is a configuration file specific to that suite. It contains `ActorName` for this particular suite. Actor is nothing else than one with specific settings and capabilities. Based on actor settings, it runs tests differently. Settings include the module's configurations and enabling modules.

tests/_support/_generated/{suite-name}TesterActions.php

This file is an auto generated file based on settings in `tests/{suite-name}.suite.yml`.

tests/_support/{suite-name}Tester.php

This file uses the generated file in the `_generated` directory and the developer can customize it more, if required. However, normally it isn't required.

tests/_support/Helper/{suite-name}.php

This file in the suite is the helper file. Here, you can add more methods in class and use that in your test cases. Just like other code has libraries and helpers, your test-cases code can also have helper methods in the helper class for that suite.

Note that you can add more files, if you need different helper classes.

Creating the API suite

In our case, we need unit tests and API tests. Although, we can use the functional tests suite for API tests because these are at the functional testing level but for the sake of clarity and understanding, we can create a separate API suite through this command:

```
composer exec codecept g:suite api
```

Here, in this command, `g` is short for generate and it will generate an API suite. `api` is just the name of another suite, and this command has created these files and directories:

```
tests/api/
tests/api.suite.yml
tests/_support/ApiTester.php
tests/_support/Helper/Api.php
tests/_support/_generated/ApiTesterActions.php
```

The `api.suite.yml` file will have basic settings without much detail. It is because the `api.suite.yml` file will have basic settings without much detail. It is because `api` here is just a name. You could even say:

```
composer exec codecept g:suite abc
```

It should have created `abc` suite with the same file structure and settings. So, our API Suite is just another test suite that we created separately for the sake of clarity and understanding.

Configuring the API suite

API needs REST client to fetch RESTful web service endpoints. Other than that it depends on Lumen. We said Lumen because it will be integrated with our code as we are writing functional level tests not acceptance tests. So, our testing framework should have insight and interaction with Lumen. What else will we need in our configuration? We need to set the testing `.env` file. So, with that here is what our configuration file looks like:

```
class_name: ApiTester
modules:
    enabled:
        - REST:
            url: /api/v1
            depends: Lumen
        - \Helper\Api
    config:
        - Lumen:
            environment_file: .env.testing
```

Before proceeding further, note that we have specified a different environment file option here under the `config/Lumen`, that is, `environment_file: .env.testing`. So, if we are specifying `.env.testing` here, then we should have a `.env.testing`. Nothing big, just copy and paste your `.env` file. From the command line, execute this:

```
cp .env .env.testing
```

Change the database credentials so that it points to the different database, having a copy of your current database schema and data, based on which you want to write test cases. Although, database-related stuff we will do during testing in Laravel/Lumen will be rollback, and will not affect our actual database, so the same database will be fine in the development. However, it is not recommended, in fact, prohibited on staging to have the same database for testing; so, better to keep different databases and configurations from the start.

We don't run tests in production. We don't even install tests related tool in production, as you can see we installed CodeCeption with the `--dev` flag. So, when our code is in production and we want to deploy a new feature, our test cases are run on a different server and then the code is deployed on the production server. There are several **CI** (**Continuous Integration**) tools available for that.

Writing test cases

Now, it's time to write test cases. The first thing is how we decide what we should test. Should we start testing every endpoint and then every class?

The first thing to understand is that we should only test the code that is written by us. By us, I mean someone from our team. We don't intend to test the code that is third-party, framework code, or a package. Also, we don't want to test each and every class and every method. In an ideal case, we can test each and every minor function's details but it has its drawbacks. First of all in the real world, we don't have time for that. We intend to test most parts but not all parts. Another reason is that all the tests that we are writing are a liability as well. We also need to maintain these tests over time. So, we do unit test for the parts where it makes sense to do so; where it is actually doing something which have some complexity. If you have a function that is as simple as that it calls another function and returns the result then I don't think that such piece of code should have its own test.

Another thing is, if we are doing unit testing as well as API testing then from where should we start writing tests? Should we write tests for all endpoints and then all classes or we will do the opposite so we will first test all classes and then all endpoints? How will we do that? We obviously intend to test our endpoints. And we also intend to test code under those endpoints. This is something that different people can do differently but I and many other people, I have seen, start writing both API tests and unit tests side by side. I prefer to write API tests and keep writing them for one resource. After that, we will go towards unit testing of controller. In our case, we don't have much stuff in the model other than what is being inherited from Eloquent or relations. During API testing of a resource, if we need more detail to fix a bug, then we can start writing unit tests for that class. But there is no hard and fast rule. It is just a matter of preference.

API tests for post resource

We can either write test cases in a structural approach or we can write it in class. Both ways are fine, I recommend class, so you can take advantage of your OOP concepts, if you want at some point. So let's create a file for that:

```
composer exec codecept generate:cest api CreatePost
```

This will create a class in `tests/api/CreatePostCest.php` with content similar to:

```php
<?php

class CreatePostCest
{
    public function _before(ApiTester $I)
```

```
        {
        }

    public function _after(ApiTester $I)
        {
        }

    // tests
    public function tryToTest(ApiTester $I)
        {
        }
    }
```

The _before() method is here so that you can write any code, which you want to execute before your test cases and the _after() method is there to execute after your test cases. The next method there is just for an example that we are going to modify.

Here, we are going to write two types of tests. One while trying to create a post without login that should returns unauthorized error and the other to create a post after login which should be successful.

Before writing that, let's set up our database factory to get random content for post, so we can use it during testing. Let's modify app/database/factories/ModelFactory.php, so it looks like this:

```
<?php

/*
|--------------------------------------------------------------------
| Model Factories
|--------------------------------------------------------------------
|
| Here you may define all of your model factories. Model factories give
| you a convenient way to create models for testing and seeding your
| database. Just tell the factory how a default model should look.
|
*/

$factory->define(App\User::class, function (Faker\Generator $faker) {
    return [
        'name' => $faker->name,
        'email' => $faker->email,
    ];
});

$factory->define(App\Post::class, function (Faker\Generator $faker) {
    return [
```

```
        'title' => $faker->name,
        'content' => $faker->text(),
        'status' => $faker->randomElement(['draft', 'published']),
    ];
});
```

The highlighted code is that I just added. So, we are telling it to return an array of parameters, title, content, and status generated through `Faker\Generator` class' object. So, based on how we have defined different fields here, we can generate random content for Post user through `ModelFactory`, so that data will be random and dynamic instead of static content. During testing, it is better to have random data in test cases to test it properly.

Okay, now let's write our test case in the `CreatePostCest.php` file, here is the function that we will write:

```
// tests if it let unauthorized user to create post
public function tryToCreatePostWithoutLogin(ApiTester $I)
{
    //This will be in console like a comment but effect nothing
    $I->wantTo("Send sending Post Data to create Post to test if it let it
created without login?");

    //get random data generated through ModelFactory
    $postData = factory(App\Post::class, 1)->make();

    //Send Post data through Post method
    $I->sendPost("/posts", $postData);

    //This one will also be like a comment in console
    $I->expect("To receive a unauthorized error resposne");

    //Response code of unauthorized request should be 401
    $I->seeResponseCodeIs(401);
}
```

As you can see, comments are explaining everything there, so there is no need to tell anything explicitly except that we have used the `sendPost()` method to send a Post request, we could also say `sendGet()` or `sendPut()` for different HTTP methods, and so on. So, now we need to run this test.

We can run it through:

```
composer exec codecept run api
```

It will not give us that clear output on the console. We can add $-v$, $-vv$, or $-vvv$ to make the output more and more verbose, but in this command, it will make composer exec-related information more and more verbose. So let's execute it as:

```
vendor/bin/codecept run api
```

Feel free to add $-v$ up to three times to get more and more verbose output:

```
vendor/bin/codecept run api -vv
```

We can make an alias of path `vendor/bin/codecept` and during that session in console, we can use shorthand like this:

```
alias codecept=vendor/bin/codecept
codecept run api -vv
```

So, execute it and you will see a lot of detail in the console. Use $-v$, $-vv$, or $-vvv$ based on how you want it. For now let's execute it as:

```
codecept run api -v
```

In our case, our first test should have passed. Now, we should write our second test case, that is, to create a post after login. It involves more things that we need to understand. So let's first see the code for this test case and then we will review it:

```php
// tests if it let unauthorized user to create post
public function tryToCreatePostAfterLogin(ApiTester $I)
{
    //This will be in console like a comment but effect nothing
    $I->wantTo("Sending Post Data to create Post after login");

    $user = App\User::first();
    $token = JWTAuth::fromUser($user);

    //get random data generated through ModelFactory
    $postData = factory(App\Post::class, 1)->make()->first()->toArray();

    //Send Post data through Post method
    $I->amBearerAuthenticated($token);
    $I->sendPost("/posts", $postData);

    //This one will also be like a comment in console
    $I->expect("To receive a unauthorized error resposne");
```

```
//Response code of unauthorized request should be 401
$I->seeResponseCodeIs(200);
```

```
}
```

If you look at this test case, you will find it very similar to the previous test case code except for a few statements. So, I have highlighted these statements in bold. The first thing is that as the test case is different, so is our `wantTo()` argument.

Then, we are getting the first user from DB and generating a token based on the user object. Here, we are calling our application code because we are using the Lumen module as configured in the `api.suite.yml` file. Then, we are using CodeCeption's `$I->amBearerAuthenticated($token)` method with `$token` that we generated. This means we are sending a valid token so the server will consider it as a logged-in user. This time response code will be 200, so by saying `$I->seeResponseCodeIs(200)`, we are telling it that it should have 200 response code or else the test should fail. That's all this code does.

Actually, there can be a lot more test cases similar to this, like test if it returns `400 Bad Request` response in case of an incomplete request.

After running tests, you will see this at the end of the console:

```
OK (2 tests, 2 assertions)
```

This shows that we are asserting two things. *Assertion means stating an expectation or fact that we want to be true.* In simple words, it is something that we are checking on response. Like, right now we are testing response code only. But in the real world, we test the whole response with a lot more test cases. CodeCeption also offers us to test those things. So, let's modify our current two test cases with more assertions. Here are two more things that we are going to test:

- Will assert that we get JSON in response.
- Will assert that we get the right data in response based on our input.

So here is our code to do so:

```php
<?php

use Tymon\JWTAuth\Facades\JWTAuth;

class CreatePostCest
{
    public function _before(ApiTester $I)
    {
```

```
        }

    public function _after(ApiTester $I)
    {
    }

    // tests if it let unauthorized user to create post
    public function tryToCreatePostWithoutLogin(ApiTester $I)
    {
        //This will be in console like a comment but effect nothing
        $I->wantTo("Send sending Post Data to create Post to test if it let
it created without login?");

        //get random data generated through ModelFactory
        $postData = factory(App\Post::class,
1)->make()->first()->toArray();

        //Send Post data through Post method
        $I->sendPost("/posts", $postData);

        //This one will also be like a comment in console
        $I->expect("To receive a unauthorized error resposne");

        //Response code of unauthorized request should be 401
        $I->seeResponseCodeIs(401);
     // Response should be in JSON format
        $I->seeResponseIsJson();
    }

    // tests if it let unauthorized user to create post
    public function tryToCreatePostAfterLogin(ApiTester $I)
    {
        //This will be in console like a comment but effect nothing
        $I->wantTo("Sending Post Data to create Post after login");

        $user = App\User::first();
        $token = JWTAuth::fromUser($user);

        //get random data generated through ModelFactory
        $postData = factory(App\Post::class,
1)->make()->first()->toArray();

        //Send Post data through Post method
        $I->amBearerAuthenticated($token);
        $I->sendPost("/posts", $postData);

        //This one will also be like a comment in console
        $I->expect("To receive a 200 response");
```

```
//Response code of unauthorized request should be 200
$I->seeResponseCodeIs(200);
// Response should be in JSON format
$I->seeResponseIsJson();

//Response should contain data that matches with request
$I->seeResponseContainsJson($postData);
    }
}
```

As you can see the highlighted text in the preceding code snippet, we have added three more assertions and you can see how simple it is. Actually, checking something in response can be tricky when we don't know what values an object can have. For example, what if we want to request and see posts list. So, how we will assert when we don't know the values? In such cases, you can use JSON path-based assertion, documented here: `http:// codeception.com/docs/modules/REST#seeResponseJsonMatchesJsonPath`. You will use it something like this:

```
$I->seeResponseJsonMatchesJsonPath('$.data[*].title');
```

This is also what you see in Response but there is even a method which tests if that record exists now in DB as well. You should try it on your own. Here you can find its documentation: `http://codeception.com/docs/modules/Db#seeInDatabase`.

Other test cases

There are a lot more test cases related to other Post operations (endpoints). However, the way to write test cases will remain same. So, I am skipping the so that you can write those test cases by yourself. However, just as a hint, here are some test cases you should write for practice:

`tryToDeletePostWithWrongId()` and it should return 404 response.

`tryToDeletePostWithCorrectId()` and it should return 200 with JSON we set there in PostController delete() method.

`tryToDeletePostWithIdBelongsToOtherUserPost()` it should return 403 Forbidden response because a user is only allowed to delete his/her own Post.

`tryToDeletePostWithoutLogin()` it should return 401 Unauthenticated because only a logged in user is allowed to delete his/her Post.

Then related to update Post:

`tryToUpdatePostWithWrongId()` and it should return 404 response.

`tryToUpdatePostWithCorrectId()` and it should return 200 with JSON having that Post data.

`tryToUpdatePostWithIdBelongsToOtherUserPost()` it should return 403 Forbidden response because a user is only allowed to update his/her own Post.

`tryToUpdatePostWithoutLogin()` and it should return 401 unauthorized.

Then related to post listing:

`tryToListPosts()` and it should return 200 response code with Post list having data and meta indices in JSON.

Then related to getting a single post:

`tryToSeePostWithId()` and it should return 200 response code with Post data in JSON.

`tryToSeePostWithInvalidId()` and it should return 404 Not Found error.

So, I would highly recommend that you write these test cases. In case you need more examples or if you want to see examples of testing authentication-related endpoints, then here you can find some examples that you can read to understand it better: `https://github.com/Haafiz/REST-API-for-basic-RPG/tree/master/tests/api`.

For more information related to CodeCeption, refer to the CodeCeption documentation at `http://codeception.com/`.

Summary

In this chapter, we learned testing types, the importance of automated testing, and wrote API tests for our RESTful web service endpoints. One thing I again want to say here is that we wrote only API tests to keep our focus on our topic but unit testing is of no less importance. However, testing is a huge topic and unit testing has its own complexity, so couldn't be discussed in this one chapter.

More resources

If you want to know more about automated testing in PHP, then here are some important resources:

Test Driven Laravel (Video course by Adam Wathan) `https://adamwathan.me/test-driven-Laravel/`, however this is mainly focused on Laravel. But still, this will teach you important things.

Similarly, there is Laravel Testing Decoded (an old book by Jeffrey Way) at `https://leanpub.com/Laravel-testing-decoded`

Again, this is a Laravel-specific book but teaches you a lot in general. There is Jeffrey Way's new upcoming book that is in general on PHP testing named Testing PHP: `https://leanpub.com/testingphp`

The preceding mentioned book that is on PHP is still not completed so you can learn from Jeffrey Way's awesome screencasts testing videos: `https://laracasts.com/skills/testing` In fact, Laracasts is not only good for testing but for learning overall PHP and Laravel.

No matter which source you pick, the important thing is that you do practice. The same is true for both development and testing. In fact, if you haven't done testing before then practicing testing is even more important. To start, you will find it a bit overwhelming but it is worth it.

9
Microservices

Although we discussed different aspects, what we have made is a RESTful web service for a simple blog in this book. We took that example to keep things simple in terms of business logic so that we can focus on our actual subject in detail. This was helpful, but in the real world, things are not that simple and small. There are big systems with different parts, which are difficult to maintain. These parts are also difficult to debug and scale. Scaling is different from just maintaining something and optimizing it for better performance. In scaling, optimization of both code and deployment environment matter. Scalability, maintainability, and performance have always been challenges that we have faced.

To handle this, we have an architectural style, known as microservices. So, in this chapter, we will discuss this. Microservices are not an essential thing to use. However, they solve some challenges that we often face while making RESTful web services for bigger systems. So, we will see how microservices solve those problems and what are the challenges that come with microservices architecture.

Here are the topics that we will discuss in this chapter:

- Introducing microservices
- Motivation towards microservices-based architecture
- How it is different from SOA (Service Oriented Architecture)
- Team structure
- Microservices challenges
- Microservices implementation

Introducing Microservices

Let's first define microservices architecture and then go into the details of microservices. Microservices architecture became a hot term, but there wasn't any formal definition. In fact, to date, there is no official consensus regarding its properties or definition. However, different people have tried to define it. I found a definition on Martin Fowler's blog very convincing. He and James Lewis defined it this way:

The microservice architectural style is an approach to developing a single application as a **suite of small services***, each* **running in its own process** *and communicating with lightweight mechanisms, often an HTTP resource API. These services are* **built around business capabilities** *and* **independently deployable** *by fully automated deployment machinery. There is a* **bare minimum of centralized management** *of these services, which may be written in different programming languages and use different data storage technologies. -- James Lewis and Martin Fowler*

It seems very formal, so let's dig into this definition and try to understand microservice architecture.

First of all, you should know that in the example, the RESTful web service we created for the blog was a monolithic web service. This means everything was in the same web service. Everything was together, so it needs to be deployed together as one code base. We can use the same monolithic approach for a bigger application as well, but that application will start becoming more and more complex and will be less scalable.

As opposed to that, microservices are composed of a lot of small services. Every small service is known as a microservice, or we can simply call it a service. These services fulfill the purpose of one application, but they are independent and very loosely coupled. So, every microservice has a separate code base and has a separate database or storage. As each microservice is independent, it can be deployed independently, even if we want to deploy on the same server or a different one. This means all services may or may not be in the same language or framework. It is possible that if one service is in PHP, another can be in Node.js and another can be in Python.

How to divide an application into microservices?

So, the question is, "If we have a big application, then how do we decide how to divide it in different micro services?" We will look into different factors while understanding how to divide one big system into microservices. These factors are based on what Martin Fowler called "Characteristics of Microservices." You can see Martin Fowler's complete post on Characteristics of Microservices at `https://martinfowler.com/articles/microservices.html`.

So, these are the factors to consider while dividing a big system into small microservices:

- Each microservice should be independent of other microservices. If not completely independent (as these services are part of one application so they may interact with each other) then dependency should be minimal.
- We will divide the application into different components. By components, we mean a unit of software that is independently replaceable and upgradeable. This means replacing or upgrading a component should not have any (or should have minimum) effect on the application. One microservice will be based on such a single component.
- A service should have a single responsibility.
- To divide an application or system into several micro-systems, you can start by looking at the business requirements. It is a good idea to make components based on business capabilities. In fact, our teams should be divided based on business capability, not based on technology.
- At the same time, it is important to ensure that services are not too fine-grained. Fine-grained services can result in more effort at the development end and still result in bad performance because there are too many things interacting with each other because they actually depend on each other.

In an ideal case, those services are always independent of each other. However, it is not always possible. Sometimes, there is something that one service needs from the other one, and sometimes, two or more services have some common logic. So, dependent services interact with each other mostly through HTTP calls, and common logic can be in a shared code base across different services. However, that is only possible when the same technology is being used in those services. Actually, this means that two or more services are depending on common code base. So, in theory based on the preceding definition, this is against the microservices architecture, but as there is no formal theory or official specification so we are considering anything that is happening in real world what is happening in the real world.

Motivation towards microservices

There are several motivations towards microservices. However, the one that I want to start with is when we are dividing it into components having single responsibilities, we are abiding by the **SRP (Single Responsibility Principle)**. Single responsibility is actually one of the first five Object Oriented Principles, also known as SOLID (`https://en.wikipedia.org/wiki/SOLID_(object-oriented_design)`). This single responsibility principle, even if it is at architectural level or low level, it makes things simple and easy. Here, in the case of microservices, separates different components from each other. So, the reason for modifying a component will be related to one single functionality. Other components and functionalities of the system will work as they were working before. This is how being separated and being independent as microservices makes them easier to modify without affecting others.

Here are some of the other reasons why it is necessary to separate microservices.

Maintenance and debugging

It is nothing new to tell that modular code is always more easily maintainable. You can debug it easily and what can be more modular than components that are not only modular but also deployed as separate modules possibly on separate servers or separate server instances. So, we get a lot of advantages out of microservices that we can get from modular code.

However, there is something to understand. If we are working with the microservices architecture from start, application will be modular because we are making services separately. However, if we didn't start with microservices and later on, we want to convert it to microservices, then first, we need to have modular code and then we can use the microservices architecture because if we don't have modules and loosely coupled code, we cannot split them in to independent components.

So, in short, motivation here for microservices is simply that we can debug modular code and components easily. In the case of maintenance, there will not be such a ripple effect if the code is in separate components and other services are getting what they need, without worrying about the internal logic of modified components.

Actually this is not it; a very important factor in the maintenance stage is productivity. In bigger code bases, productivity can be reduced over time, because developers need to worry about the whole application. However, in microservices, developers in one team doing one particular change don't have to worry about the whole application but the code inside that particular service at the time, because for that particular change and for the developer working on it, this one microservice is the whole application which has a lot less responsibility than the overall application. So, that way, productivity during maintenance can be much better in microservices than monolithic applications.

Scalability

When your system scales and you want to serve more clients and want good performance as well, after sometime, when you have done optimizations as well, you need better, more powerful servers. You can make servers more powerful by adding more resources into them. This is called vertical scaling. Vertical scaling has its limits. After all, this is one server. What if we want more scalability? Actually, there is another way of scaling, that is, horizontal scaling. In horizontal scaling, you add more small servers or server instances instead of adding all the resources in to one server. In that case, how will one monolithic application be deployed on multiple servers? We will probably need to deploy the complete application on multiple servers and then load balancers, managing traffic through multiple servers.

However, having the whole application on multiple servers is not cost effective. What if we can have one part of the application served from one server and another part from another server? How can this be possible? We have one application. So, this is where the microservices architecture comes in. Its advantages are not limited to just scalability. One of its key benefits is the loosely coupled components of a system.

Technology diversity

As we have seen, in microservices, every codebase is separate from the other. So, different teams working on different services can use different technologies and different storage if they want to. In fact, those teams are completely free from the need to use the same technology across different services until you are providing other services that are interacting with each other. However, if we want to use the option of shared code to avoid repeatedly writing the same logic in different technologies, then to have a shared code base, we may need to use the same technology.

Resilience

In microservices, resilience is also one of the key benefits. As every service is a separate component, if one component of the system is failing for some reason, then the problem can be isolated from the rest of the system.

However, we need to make sure that with failures, the system degrades properly. If there is failure in a service, we can try to minimize it, but there can be a failure again. However, to minimize its effect, we should handle it carefully so that we minimize its impact on other services and our application's user.

Replaceability

If you want to replace a part of the system, then it is not that simple in monolithic architecture because everything is in the same code base. However, in microservices, it is easier to replace one component of the system because all you need to do is have another service and replace it with the existing one. Obviously, you still need to have an alternative service, but it is not like replacing the whole component in the same code base with some other code.

Parallelization

Normally, clients want their software to be developed early and come onto the market early so that they can test their idea or capture more market. For that reason, they want more developers working in parallel on their application. Unfortunately, in monolithic applications, we can do limited parallel work. Actually, we can do that in monolithic applications as well if we have very modular code. However, still, it can't be as independent and modular as it is in a microservices-based application.

Every service is being developed and deployed separately. Although these services communicate with each other, still, development can be done independently, and in most cases, we can keep several services being developed separately. So, many developers, in fact, the development team, can work in parallel, which means software can be developed early. If there is a problem or another feature is required in multiple modules, then it can be done in parallel.

How it is different from SOA

SOA stands for Service Oriented Architecture. By name it seems that this architecture depends on services just like micro-services. Service Orientation is a design paradigm in computer software in the form of services. Its principles stress the separation of concerns (the same as SRP). Until now, it seems similar to microservices. Before understanding difference, we need to know that what is SOA. Although there is no one clear official definition of SOA. So let's take this basic definition from wikipedia:

> *A service-oriented architecture (SOA) is a style of software design where services are provided to the other components by application components, through a communication protocol over a network. The basic principles of service-oriented architecture are independent of vendors, products and technologies.*

If you look at this definition then you will find that SOA is very similar to micro-services but its definition is not that concise and clear. One reason can be that SOA itself is a generalized architecture. Or we can better say that SOA is generalized form of micro-services.

As stated in Oracle's post:

> *Microservices are the kind of SOA we have been talking about for the last decade. -- Torsten Winterberg, Oracle ACE Director.*

So micro-services follow same principles but it is bit more specialized and focus on having multiple independent services where a service is a completely different component and it exists independent of other services.

Team structure

As per Conway's law:

> *"Organizations which design systems ... are constrained to produce designs which are copies of the communication structures of these organizations."*

So, in order to produce designs based on microservices architecture and to gain its benefits, we also need structured teams working on this accordingly.

Normally, in a monolithic application, we have teams such as the following ones:

- Dev-ops team
- Backend-developer team
- DB administrator team
- Mobile application developer team

However, in the case of distributed architecture such as microservices (if we are developing an e-commerce application), we will have teams such as the following ones:

- Products catalog
- Inventory
- Orders
- Coupons
- Wishlist

All these teams will have members, including Dev-ops, Backend-developer, DB administrator, and mobile app developer. So, in the case of microservices, we will have a team per service.

Size of team:

There is no hard and fast rule, but it is recommended that team size should be as per Jeff Bezos' 2 pizza rule: *if a team couldn't be fed with two pizzas, it was too big.* The reason is that if the team becomes bigger, then communication can be terrible.

Challenges of micro-services

Nothing comes free. Everything has its downside or at least some challenges that you need to deal with. If we go for microservices, it has its own challenges. So, let's look at them and discuss how they can be minimized if there is trade-off.

Infrastructure maintenance

Although you don't have to update your infrastructure every day, it still needs to be maintained and it needs more effort. Technology freedom comes with microservices, but not without any cost. You have to maintain different server instances using different technologies. This will need better infrastructure and people with experience of more technologies.

Actually, you don't always need better infrastructure and people with knowledge of all those different technologies. Normally, every team working on different services will have its own infrastructure or Dev-ops-related people. However, in that case, you need more people because now, you are not sharing Dev-ops or infrastructure-related people across different teams. In fact, this is how teams are made for microservices. Teams don't have shared resources at-least they shouldn't have. Otherwise, you don't get the advantage of parallel working because of independent services.

However, infrastructure doesn't only mean server setup, but also deployments, monitoring, and logging. So, for that purpose, you can't just use one technology and solve the problem on the trade-off of limiting your technology choices. However, limiting your technology choices can make it a bit easier for Dev-ops as well.

Another thing is that you need to have automated deployments on a continuous integration server. It runs your test cases, and then, if everything works well, it deploys on your actual server. For this purpose, you need to have Dev-ops person/people who write scripts to automate your deployments. There are several ways to do so.

Performance

Actually, there can be reasons for microservices to run faster if one completely independent microservice is being used by the client. A clear reason is that a request has to go through less stuff in one small micro-service than passing through a big monolithic application.

However, this is an ideal case and not all microservices are completely independent of each other. They interact with each other and depend on each other. So, if one service has to get something from another one, it will most probably need a network call, and network calls are expensive. This results in performance problems. However, this can be minimized if services are created in a way where dependency is minimal. If dependency is not minimal, that means services are not independent and in that case we can combine such services and make one independent service.

Another option can be shared code; the code that will be used across different services. If two or more services are using the same functionality, then instead of having that as another service that different services depend on, we can simply make it a shared code that will be part of different services' code base. We will not repeat ourselves and will try to make it a module or package that different services can use. However, some people think it is bad practice as we will have some code shared between different services, which means it is not going to be loosely coupled.

Debugging and fault-finding

As you can see, we said debugging and maintenance will be easier in a microservice. However, it also becomes a challenge when there is communication between these services and one's output is effecting another.

When we have different services, we need a way for services to communicate with each other. Services communicate with each other in two ways: through HTTP calls or through messages. Here, by messages we mean using some sort of messaging queues such as RabbitMQ and so on. In the case of message passing, it can be very difficult if there is some bug or something unexpected is happening. Since it is not one service and every service is working based on the previous service's output, it is difficult to know where the problem is.

So, a way to tackle this is to write tests thoroughly. Because if it is making sure that every service's test cases are written and testing whether they are working fine, then it can fail before deployment.

However, this is not always the case. It is because there is not one service. Many services are interacting and sometimes, there is a problem in the live environment and you want to debug and fix it. For this purpose, logs are very important. However, again, this is a distributed environment. So, what can we do? Here are few things that you need to ensure you do with logs.

Logs should be centralized

You need to collect logs in some central place. If you have logs in one centralized place, then it is much easier to look into them instead of checking every server instance for its logs.

It is also important because you should have logs in an external place other than your instances as logs' backup. The reason is that if you replace an instance, then you probably want to keep a copy of your logs to utilize while debugging. This can be any place either Amazon S3, your DB, or a disk, but you want it to be durable and available. If you are on AWS, then you can also use their monitoring service named CloudWatch at `https://aws.amazon.com/cloudwatch/`.

Logs should be searchable

Having logs is good. But just like a lot of information on Internet, it is not really useful if you don't know which link has the right information for you. It has become easier because of search engines telling us which pages have more relevant content. Similarly, logs of live applications, especially when there is a log of many services together, will not be that helpful. There will be a lot of logs. So, in order to make them usable, you should store your logs in way in which they can be searched for and be easily understood when you see them.

Track chain of requests

Just like users go from one page to another on a website, the users' clients send request after request to perform different tasks. So, it is a good idea to know which requests the user sent before this one because in some cases, previous requests can have an impact othes. So, to track this, you can simply pass an identifier for the first time and should expect the same among all other requests.

Another advantage is that it will not only show you flow, but it will also be easier for you if you are asked to explain why some specific problem occurred. If that identifier is at the client side, the concerned person can give you that identifier for reference with their error report so that you can can understand which request flow to trace.

Dynamic log levels

Normally, for logging, you use some sort of logging framework, and typical log levels are warning, info, debug, and verbose. Normally, in production, log level info or other information is used, but if you want to have some problem and you want to debug it, you should be able to dynamically change that log level.

So, if you need, you should be able to set the log level dynamically on the fly. This is important because if you have problems in production, then you don't want it to persist for a long time.

Implementation

As this chapter is just an introduction to microservices, we will not go into the details of implementation. However, we will just have an overview of how we will implement different things in microservices. We have already discussed RESTful web service implementation in this book. However, here are some other pieces that come with microservices. So, we will just get idea of what is involved in implementing these parts.

Deployments

We will have deployments automated. We will use continuous delivery tools. Continuous delivery is a process in which there are frequent deliveries with short cycles, and it ensures that software can be reliably released at any time. It aims to release software faster and minimize risk with a build, and test and release software frequently approach.

Continuous delivery takes automation from source control all the way through production. There are various tools or processes that help in accomplishing a continuous delivery process. However, two important things in this are as follows:

- Testing
- CI (Continuous Integration)

First of all, before committing to code, a developer should run their tests (most importantly, unit tests) while on commit CI server, run integration tests, and integrate on the CI server if tests are passed. Travis CI and Jenkins CI are popular CI tools. Other than that, Circle CI is popular as well.

After continuous integration, build is made automatically and deployed automatically. As a picture is worth a thousand words, to elaborate further, I have added this image from Wikipedia here (this image is from Wikimedia):

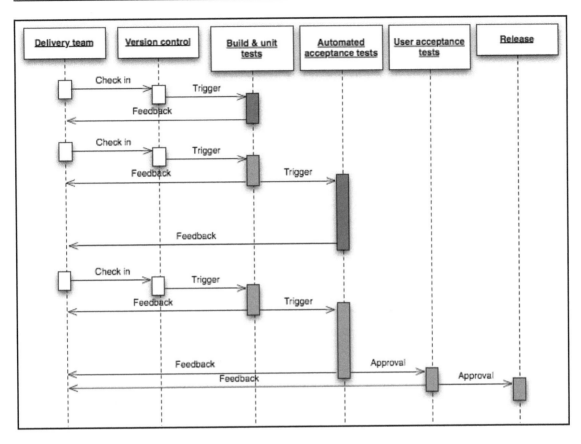

Through this diagram, we will get some idea of CI. For detailed information on continuous delivery, you can read the Wikipedia article at `https://en.wikipedia.org/wiki/Continuous_delivery`.

Inter-services communication

We saw that communication between servers is important. Services depend on each other, and sometimes, input of one service is the output of another, while sometimes, one service is using another. One important thing is communication between these services.

So, we can divide inter-service communication into two types:

1. Synchronous communication
2. Asynchronous communication

Synchronous communication

In synchronous communication, one service communicates with another and waits to get a result. This is normally done through simple HTTP calls using the same approach as end clients. So, these are simple HTTP calls that get a response (mostly JSON). One service sends an HTTP request to another service, waits for its response, and proceeds after getting the response. Synchronous communication has network overheads and have to wait for response, but it is simple to implement and sometimes that delay is not a problem. So in such cases, for the sake of simplicity we can use synchronous communication.

Asynchronous communication

In asynchronous communication, one service doesn't wait for another's response. It is based on a pub-sub model. It uses a message broker to send messages to other consumer/subscriber's services. It is done using Lightweight Messaging tools, through which one service sends messages to another. Such messaging tools include, but are not limited to, RabbitMQ, Apache Kafka, and Akka.

If you are interested in knowing more about microservices inter communications, then the article at http://howtocookmicroservices.com/communication/ might seem interesting.

Shared library or common code

As we discussed, there can be some code that is common among different services. It can be third-party code as well as code written by teams for the same application. In either case, we obviously want to use that common code. In order to do that, we don't just replicate that code in our applications because it breaks the DRY (Don't Repeat Yourself) principle. However, note that we can't use common code if we are using different programming languages/technologies.

So what we do is, we package that common code or shared library and upload it somewhere, from where we can fetch that package while deploying it. In the case of PHP, we will create composer packages and upload at packagist. Then, in service, when we need that common code, we will simply install the composer's package and use that common code from the vendor directory.

Such packages and package managers like composer are not just in PHP. In Node.js, there is NPM (Node Package Manager) using which you can create a Node package to serve the purpose. So, in different technologies, there are different ways to create and use such packages.

Summary

In this chapter, as the last chapter of this book, I tried to introduce microservices, an architecture style getting a lot of attention nowadays. We looked into it because we needed an architecture in which we can use RESTful web services to achieve better performance and scalability in complex and bigger systems.

The focus of the book was RESTful web services in PHP7, and we looked at other topics that were connected with building RESTful web services or PHP7 in someway. We looked at some of these topics in detail, whereas we just touched upon some others. Many of these topics are too broad to be contained in one chapter. Some of these topics can have a complete book dedicated to them. That's why, I provided different URLs towards learning material or suggested reading, which you can refer to if you are interested.

What's next

There are two important things:

Practice:

Actual learning starts when you start practicing something. When you practice, you sometimes face problems and learn more, which you couldn't learn without solving those problems.

Looking into suggested material:

Wherever I have provided suggested reading, pause there and at least have a look at the suggested material. If you find it helpful, feel free to dig deeper into it. Who knows, that suggested material might teach you something even more valuable to you than this entire book. After all, that material provides much more detail than we have discussed in this book.

Index

Lightning Source UK Ltd.
Milton Keynes UK
UKHW03f0615180518
322796UK00011B/289/P

9 781787 127746